Our Interrupted Fairy Tale

A TRUE STORY

Megan Williams

Publication Data

Megan Williams
Our Interrupted Fairy Tale
ISBN-10: 1493712616
ISBN-13: 9781493712618

Manufactured in the United States of America

Editor: Lori Bamber
Cover design by: Kait Jones

"I want to thank all of you survivors out there. It's you who keep the hope alive for those who are newly diagnosed or in the midst of their battle."

Chad Warren

DEDICATION

For Chad

ACKNOWLEDGEMENTS

To our families and friends,
to Chad's bone marrow donor and amazing health care team —
and to everyone else who loved and supported us on this journey.

PROLOGUE

Thursday Oct 29, 2009

To my groom, to my other half,

You, sir, are one of a kind.

You are one of the kindest, most generous people I have ever known and you make me feel like a princess.

You have handled the curve balls that life has thrown at you with strength, discipline, courage and determination. Yet you also tell stories that put people at complete ease and make them laugh so hard they cry, or leave them thinking, "Did he really just say that?"

I love you. I cannot tell you in words how proud you make me, how much I admire you, how often you are in my thoughts and how much your love has changed me forever.

To the man who owns my heart—I look forward to the next seven decades. To being your wife, listening to your stories, loving you and—of course—making fun of you.

26 IS TOTALLY OLD

Megan

I couldn't stop watching him.

He stood across from me at the back of Court 3 in baggy, grey sweat pants, with a relaxed confidence that made him seem approachable, but maybe a bit too cool for those of us in tennis whites.

He swung a perfect forehand stroke at any ball that was hit in his direction. Then he would saunter to the back of the court, giving enough space for the others around him to take their turn. I couldn't tell if he was friends with the people he was playing tennis with, or if he was just friendly. Those who stood near were included in his smiles, his jokes—and his cough.

I wondered how old he was. He's old, but how old? And why isn't he wearing tennis clothes like the rest of us? With that cough, why doesn't he just sit down?

It was a rainy April weekend in North Vancouver, and my Dad and I were taking our tennis instructor certification at the Grant Connell Tennis Centre. There were 20 of us taking the course, but Chad was the only one I was curious about.

"I'm Chad," he said when it was his turn to introduce himself to the group. I sat beside my dad, waiting for the circle of introductions to come around to me. Chad. A pretty simple name for someone who didn't seem so simple to figure out, especially for my 16-year-old self. "I'm Megan," I said, working hard not to look over at him in case he was looking at me.

When I heard my dad say, "I'm Tony," I thought it was safe to look in Chad's direction again.

Big, soft, brown eyes smiled back at me. We shared a smile before I looked away and made a deliberate effort to seem interested in listening to Michael, Kyle, Jason and David introduce themselves.

Unlike the rest of the group, who all seemed keen to learn, Chad's posture made me think he wasn't all that interested in being there. At the same time, he seemed interested in what we tennis dorks had to say.

The course was three weekends, over two months. And for the days he was there, Chad showed up in his sweat pants, shared a few laughs with people he seemed to know, hit a few balls, and coughed. When he wasn't there, I wasn't sure if I was disappointed or simply curious to know what better things he had to do. Whatever it was, I noticed his absence.

On the last weekend of the course, during a lunch break, Dad and I were sitting at a wire table at the far end of the food court when we spotted Chad scouting out a table, balancing Chinese food and a sports drink on his tray. Dad caught his attention and offered a chair. *He's old; I have to behave,* I thought. But in the end, it didn't matter how I acted. Chad and my dad carried the half-hour conversation. I just sat, listened, and tried to make plenty of eye contact with my food so as not to stare for too long.

Chad light-heartedly briefed us on why he had missed time at the course and why he was coughing so much. "It's pneumonia, and it doesn't seem to be getting better. I've been coughing so much I've cracked a rib."

I learned he was trying to get back into tennis and coaching after spending five years at Southeastern Louisiana University on a tennis scholarship. He was 26.

Ten years older than me! Like a decade! That means he's already done university—26 is totally old.

Then he began to direct questions at me: When did I start playing tennis? Who were my coaches? Any plans after I graduated? What tournaments was I playing? He listened to my answers with genuine interest. I, on the other hand, could not remember a single sentence of what I said, and was grateful every time my dad spoke up and endorsed my improving backhand.

I liked his company, and for some reason I felt lucky to spend that time with him. I liked that he had revealed details about himself and made an effort to learn a little about us too.

But, as expected, when the course ended a day later, we went our respective ways. I knew it was unlikely I would see Chad again.

A week later my junior-tennis friend Alyssa called. "Hey—did you meet a guy named Chad at the coaching course you were just at?" she asked.

It turned out that she worked at a local tennis court with Chad, and had wondered if the tennis-coaching course he'd mentioned attending was the same one I'd told her about earlier.

"Yeah," I replied.

"Well, he just walked in and quit. He's been diagnosed with cancer."

"*What?!* What kind of cancer?"

"Something to do with his blood," Alyssa explained.

I was sitting on the deck with my dad, who was eavesdropping while reading the paper. When I hung up and repeated the news, all he said was "Ah, shit."

My dad hardly ever swore.

IS IT TERMINAL?

Chad

So much has happened that it's hard to know where to start but I'm just going to let it flow.

My health has been questionable over the last year or so, and I had a few memorable, intense illnesses. Prior to that, I had lived my life free of any sickness beyond the occasional cold.

One day, a flu knocked me out bad enough that I went to a local clinic for a checkup. I was told I had pneumonia and that my family doctor would run some tests.

You never know when to stop. I dragged myself off the tennis court in the middle of a lesson to go see the doctor that day. Who knew that it would be the start of the rest of my life?

At first they found I had an enlarged heart with an irregular beat. Then my doctor called me at about 10:30 at night to tell me that I had to see a specialist the next morning. There was talk that I might have leukemia, so for a week it was a possibility—I was scared. I had a bone marrow biopsy that week and was scheduled to meet with the specialist to discuss the results. I worked that morning, and met my mother for the appointment at noon.

Dr. Boldt invited me in. The office was empty. There were no other patients and the receptionist had gone to lunch. (I guess they thought we might cause a scene and shoot the place up!)

I went in alone and I can't say that I remember anything she said. She went over my results and then bang, out it came; that feared word. Cancer.

I called my mother in to hear what Dr. Boldt was saying while I broke down in the hall. All I remember Mom asking was, "Is it terminal?"

On May 17, 2001, at 26 years old, I was diagnosed with a cancer of the bone marrow called multiple myeloma. It is extremely rare in people under 30. In fact, there are almost no statistics on young people with this disease.

My mom had to lie down in Dr. Boldt's office.

As for me, I think my mind was blown the moment I heard the word cancer.

I thought of Katharine, my girlfriend. How was I supposed to tell the most important person in my life, a woman who had recently lost her brother, that I have cancer?

Jay Sedgwick, Katharine's brother, was a close friend of mine who had died of testicular cancer a little more than two years before.

I remembered receiving the news from his sister Kristen and crying in my mother's arms.

I had just been to see Jay several hours earlier. He was very tired, but at his 24th birthday celebration the day before he looked the best he had in months. He was sitting up in bed, grinning ear-to-ear, holding up a pink piece of paper. It was ownership papers to his dad's Eagle Talon sports car, which he loved. Now it was his, and I could see the excitement in his eyes. It was an amazing day, and everyone was there—his sisters, friends, parents, aunts and uncles.

I left that day firmly believing he was going to make it. He had already made it through multiple operations that he wasn't expected to have survived.

Before one major operation, his mother had called his close friends to his bedside one at a time so that he could say his good-byes. I don't know what he said to everyone, but to me he said, "Thank you for being a good friend."

I was so overwhelmed by the whole thing that I didn't know what to say. I just wanted to hug him and cry.

The day after his birthday, Jay wasn't the same, but I gave him a kiss on the cheek and said I would be back the next day to watch a movie with him. I never saw him again.

We had a celebration of his life the following week at the Hollyburn Country Club. The turnout was brilliant and really showed the kind of person he was. By no means did it bring closure to it all. There never will be closure to his death. I just hope I can keep the positives of his life in my memory, and that he knew how much I truly cared about him.

The day of my diagnosis, I picked Katharine up from work and held her and cried as I told her my news. She has been by my side through the whole thing. People told me that cancer can tear relationships apart because of the stress. Not us. Sure, we have had our ups and downs, but we are truly in love. Despite the luck we have had over the past few years, we are happy just living each day together.

I'm not sure I can put into words the feelings that came over me in the days and weeks following my diagnosis but maybe the closest thing would be…euphoria!?

I stopped working the day I was diagnosed with a disease that usually hits people over 60, and began treatment the next day. I was immediately put on a high dose of steroids and a bone-strengthening IV once a month.

Blood cancers are very complicated, and to this day I don't understand half the terminology, but multiple myeloma affects cells in the bone marrow, weakening the bones, immune system and the rest of the body.

I was sent to the specialists at the VGH Bone Marrow Transplant Unit, where I've spent much of my time since being diagnosed. Since I was so young and have such an aggressive cancer, the treatment was also aggressive. I was told that my best chance at an extended life was a bone marrow transplant. *(Huh? How do they cut into every bone and shoot marrow into you?!)* I was put on a worldwide transplant list and the search for a match to my bone marrow began, as did my euphoric summer.

Work had been getting tougher even during the months leading up to my diagnosis, and was now out of the question. I had bone pain throughout my rib cage. I had broken ribs just by playing tennis, and was unable to sleep because of the pain. I had bouts of pneumonia. I was coming apart at the seams.

I was lucky all my debts were insured, and I didn't have to pay them while I was sick. I collected employment insurance, and my family helped out when needed.

I waited for a donor.

It was a very strange time. My sister was tested but was not a match. I knew I had at least three months of taking each day and living it to its fullest. I developed an enormous appetite from the steroids, and I looked forward to each meal. I began playing golf almost every day.

I drove Katharine to work every morning at 7:00, and that's when my day began. I cleaned the house, then found someone to go to brunch with. After, I golfed or went on long motorcycle rides. I continued working out, using much lighter weights, at a pace that I felt my body could handle.

My life became about one thing: enjoying every moment. The steroids made me feel better fast, but it's not real. They actually weaken you, make you crazy and really, really hungry.

The summer of 2001 was particularly hot, and I enjoyed each moment of it. After afternoons of golf or motorcycle rides, I waited for Katharine to get off work so we could begin the evening festivities.

It seems like we'd have our friends over to barbecue salmon, eat cherries, and laugh the night away every night. We smoked plenty of pot, which really helped me wind down from the steroids and keep my mind off things. The support of our friends and family played (and continues to play) a crucial role in getting through it.

Fitness and sports have always been a large part of my life, and I wanted to go into my transplant as fit as possible without overdoing it. I would do a weight circuit and 15 to 20 minutes on the stair master at least three or four times a week. It made me feel normal to keep that part of my life going. Since I was no longer working, I had nothing but time to think and prepare.

Katharine and I became closer than ever.

Any girl who could put up with me, especially during that time, has to be very special and patient person.

The steroids gave me incredible mood swings, and I gave Katharine a hard time. She never held it against me; she just kept loving me.

I found it difficult to wind down to sleep, so I began using marijuana nightly. I would recommend it to anyone in the same situation. I may have taken it to the extreme over those few months, but there were lots of laughs and it mellowed me out. It was a big help, especially in keeping my mind from what I call the dark shadows.

The "dark shadows" were the feelings I had the moment I was diagnosed. Any time my mind started to wander, the dark shadows carried me into hell. I don't want to die, and it is a strong possibility.

Eventually, I began to accept the fact that death can happen at any time to anyone. I may be staring down the barrel of a gun, but it hasn't gone off. Those dark shadows come and go, but I've learned to deal with them better.

What scared me more than death was the thought of not growing old with Katharine. It hurts so intensely I still can't bear to write about it. It is my mission to prevent that from happening. I am and always will be a survivor.

Katharine and I had an amazing couple of months before my transplant. As the summer went on, I became more and more free, like I had detached from the world, floating away like a balloon.

I hadn't a care in the world except riding my bike and when the next joint would be lit. Katharine and I took off to my favorite place in B.C., Penticton, for a few days of even more "chillin."

We rented one of those semi-detached cabins near Skaha Lake, and got into our routine: a little breakfast, light workout, stroll to the beach, puffing on a doob. Then we hit up one of P-town's many attractions: batting cages, go carts and beach bikes. We loved it all!

The weather was gorgeous. I wasn't supposed to be in the sun because of some potent antibiotic I was on, but I didn't obey, and we were at the lake every day.

One afternoon, while lying on Skaha Beach, I checked my messages. There was a voicemail from my doctor.

When I called back, the lady from the bone marrow transplant program told me they had found a donor. I was to be admitted on August 8 to begin three days of chemotherapy and then three days of total body radiation.

My transplant was scheduled for the night of August 15.

It's funny—it never even crossed my mind that they might not find a donor, which is the case for too many people. I don't think I was thinking, period. But in that moment, everything changed again. I was thinking. It's really happening—it isn't a dream. And I have to deal with it.

DO NOT FALL IN LOVE WITH
AN AMERICAN

In grade 12, my evenings were spent at the tennis club. Once in a while, I'd ask about Chad, hoping someone had heard that he—well, that he hadn't died.

The tennis scene in Vancouver is very tight-knit. If you haven't played against someone, you've likely coached with them or, at the very least, seen them at a tournament. Though Chad was a veteran, and known by many, no one had heard anything; it was as though he had vanished.

Eventually, I just stopped asking. My 17-year-old life was becoming the only thing I could think of. Though I hadn't thought past my prom dress, my parents had taken the advice of one of my coaches and urged me to get a tennis scholarship.

After graduation, more practices were set up; universities were researched. Videos were filmed and packaged off to schools offering full scholarships for women's tennis.

Less than six months after "tennis scholarship" was initially suggested, my mom and I were on a plane to the University of

Wyoming where I would be playing for the Division 1 Women's Tennis Team.

There was a lot that went into making it happen for me, yet when we arrived at the airport, Dad held back tears as he said goodbye and left me with one simple instruction: "*Do not* fall in love with an American."

16 MONTHS TO LIVE

My time of just living each day was coming to an end. As much as I tried to continue our endless summer, it wasn't the same. In a few short weeks I was about to get very sick, maybe even die.

I was scared. I worried about Katharine, and about entering unknown territory.

I was going into the hospital for some indefinite amount of time, and facing a much longer recovery period. I was told I would be out of commission for a year, which seemed unreal to me. Those who have been through these sorts of things know what I'm talking about when I say they lay it all out for you.

You have to do test after test, interviews with doctors feeding you every stat available. I suppose it's protocol, but how many times do you need to tell someone the mortality rate of the procedure or disease? I know I'm sick. Please just tell me about the people who survived and are living a normal life... *That's all anyone wants to hear!*

Like anyone would be, I was very uneasy about what was going to happen to me. The risks were great, and the doctors let me know, over and over. Basically they were giving enough chemo and radiation to kill me. Then they perform the transplant, which hopefully keeps and goes on to save my life.

I tried not to listen to the survival rates. I found it took me a week to recover after a meeting with a doctor. Each visit took away my hope. Ask anyone who has cancer, and they will tell you: hope is the only thing we have left.

I heard them say that I had a 50 percent chance of surviving through the first year after the transplant. I was told that the whole reason for the transplant was to extend my life longer than a few years. Untreated, they said I had 16 months to live so—at the time—five or ten years extra sounded pretty good. Everything was happening so fast; I didn't know what to think.

I met with a doctor who explained all the complications that could occur later in life, courtesy of the radiation. A major and immediate effect, because I would receive such a high dose of radiation, is that I'd be sterile for life.

Fortunately, my mother booked me an appointment at a fertility clinic, where I managed to fill six straws, which I assume gives Katharine and I six chances to have kids when the time comes. Six chances are better than no chances at all, and having kids is definitely something I have always dreamed of, so this was something positive out of such a potential negative.

But the doctor rattled off a whole list of other potential physical ailments that I am at high risk for because of the radiation. What I have gone through can't be reversed, and I find that tough to swallow. I have put my life in the hands of a few doctors, and can only hope they are up to date on all the latest treatments.

It is my life.

Researching my cancer is my job.

But this disease is so frustrating, because there is no cure yet.

I arrived at the hospital on August 8, 2001, a gorgeous summer day. In the morning, just before I was admitted, Katharine's dad Brian had booked me a private introductory flying lesson in a small plane out in Ladner. I had spent a fair amount of time with Brian, riding motorcycles all over the city, and enjoyed being around him. We'd become friends.

Anyways, there I was, flying over the city in this tiny little plane. We had a great time, but my mind was on the hospital, so I don't know if I fully appreciated it. I'll never forget it, but it was hard to fully enjoy it knowing that, in a few hours, I was facing hell.

Part of me wanted to get on with it, the other wanted to hop on my motorbike with Katharine on the back and ride away.

Not more than an hour after we landed, I walked through the doors of VGH, where I was to spend the next month. It was the hardest thing I've ever dealt with in my life.

I started by receiving total body radiation twice a day for three days, a strange experience because the effects of that shit are irreversible. It alone reduced my lung capacity to 70 percent at best. The next three days I received lethal-dose chemotherapy, which means they gave me the max amount of chemo my body could handle without it killing me. The combination brings all your counts to zero, so you have no blood cells or immune system to fight the donor marrow.

I would have trouble for the rest of my life with the effects of the total body radiation I endured. It was like I was being burned from the inside out; my skin peeled for months after. My lung capacity was damaged, significantly and permanently, and a whole bunch of other permanent shit that you don't wish on anyone. But it's what had to be done if I wanted to stay alive.

I handled the chemo very well, and as disturbing as the radiation was, I dealt with that too. I took on every chemical and drug they threw at me. Don't get me wrong, I felt terrible and could barely eat at all.

My hair fell out about two weeks into my stay, and I was quarantined in my room for 23 days. That was the hardest part: not being able to leave my room because my blood counts went to zero while they waited for my new bone marrow to graft.

Each day felt longer than the one before and, of course, I began to get weaker each day also. A nurse came in every hour to check on me. After a while, I looked forward to it. I had plenty of visitors, usually in the evening. Of course Katharine was there plenty, and having her there got me through it.

I enjoyed my parents' daily visits, which were short but very important to me. They brought me food that my stomach could handle. I stopped getting the hospital trays halfway through my stay. Some days, all I could eat was ice cream and popsicles. I tried hard to keep eating because if I didn't, they would start me on intravenous feeding. You have a much easier go of things if you can keep eating.

The transplant happened at midnight, and was fairly anticlimactic. I had a Hickman line into my chest where I received all my medications, chemo, and then my transplant.

A doctor and a nurse entered my room to monitor me and hung what looked like a bag of blood: my new marrow, which took about 45 minutes to drip through.

My mother was there with Katharine. I was heavily medicated, but I still remember being very nervous, as were my mother and Katharine, who played cards to pass the time.

As the days passed, the chemo and radiation began to take effect, and I became weaker and weaker. The staff was amazing, as was my support group, but you have to dig deep. You have to stay strong.

I busted out of there in 31 days, but I spent the next several months going to and from the VGH BMT (Bone Marrow Transplant) day clinic.

I'd lost 30 pounds and couldn't do a single push up, not to mention had no blood counts. Yet I was so eager to ride a motorcycle on my first day out that I borrowed Brian's Harley and managed to ride it to the clinic for my treatment. The nurses and doctors were not impressed, but I was happy ripping down the highway at full throttle.

Now I was in control.

READY TO MOVE ON

Katharine was amazing through it all and we had a lot of support, but I needed rest. There were some scares early on, the most noteworthy about a month after I left the hospital. My blood counts began crashing, back down to zero. My doctor told me it was one of two things: the transplant had failed or the cancer had come back. Either way, I was done.

So, having just heard that my time had run out, I had to have another bone marrow biopsy to confirm. They are quite unpleasant, especially when you are feeling unwell. They stick a large needle into the top of your hip, deep into the core, to extract a sliver of bone marrow so they can test to see what the cancer is doing. It takes all the doc's strength to drive that thing in there, and it takes your breath away once they're in. I've had so many over the years, and they still get me clammy.

It would be a week of waiting for confirmation. I don't even remember my frame of mind anymore, as I think I went numb. I finally got the call—would you believe there was a third option? Just a viral infection.

All was fine. It was just a setback. I love my doctor, who has kept me alive for all these years, going above and beyond with me as he does with all his patients. I'd do anything for him, but this experience opened my eyes to the fact that doctors don't have all the answers.

This was new territory for them as well. I was one of the youngest people to be diagnosed with multiple myeloma, which seems to be really aggressive and unpredictable with us young folk.

I had so many chemicals running through me. I didn't realize until much later just how long they take to wear off. Five months after my transplant, I've finally started to feel like me again. I find it harder to talk about the past because I'm feeling ready to move on, and this makes me remember the bad times.

A FEW LINGERING PROBLEMS

Over the next several months, I continued recovery, rehabbing my body slowly, starting with a few push-ups once per week, then incorporating total body exercises with some light dumbbells I had at home.

I did some walking, and around Christmas I started back at the gym doing what I could. I was determined to be strong and healthy again, but I trained like my life depended on it…!?

I was so intense. I never spoke to anyone and I remember getting emotional almost every workout. The problem was that my body couldn't handle what I was doing to it, so I was always getting sick and having to start over. It was trying to recover and accept the new bone marrow, and I was making it repair and grow muscle.

I was young, and had to learn that moderation would take time and lots of trial and error. I would never be the same after the transplant—it took a piece of me—but I have high expectations for myself.

About six months post-transplant, I began working a few hours a week coaching tennis, which proved vital in helping me begin to get out and come alive again. I assisted with the competitive junior groups at the North Shore Winter Club, where I had coached before my diagnosis. We had all the best juniors in the province, which made it fun, and I began hitting in with them.

Even before I got sick, it had been years since I played tennis with any real focus. Even during college I had lost my love for it. I did what I had in order to keep my scholarship, but nothing more.

Now I was pretty rusty, but focused on improving. Being so passionate about getting better made me a better coach—I could transfer that passion to them, and it felt good interacting. I began to really enjoy tennis again.

It has now been 15 months since my transplant and I have a few lingering problems. I am improving.

But this year has brought more trauma: both my parents were diagnosed with cancer. As I write, my mother is fighting for her life. She also has multiple myeloma.

Dad had his kidney removed and doctors are confident they got all the cancer out. Four weeks after surgery, he hiked to the top of a mountain, and to this day he never really speaks of it.

WHAT'S GOING ON?

I was only 19, and I had already had enough. Three semesters on the University of Wyoming's NCAA Division 1 Women's Tennis Team, and I couldn't take it anymore.

I wasn't happy; I didn't like where I was or who I was.

Once I mustered up the confidence to tell my coach I had decided that I wouldn't be returning to the team, or to Wyoming for my junior year, I was shunned.

Within hours my teammates, who I believed had become my closest friends, gave me the silent treatment. I guessed my coach suggested they no longer speak to me, but I couldn't decide if it was more hurtful that she would do that or that my friends had obeyed.

Though there were only two months left in the school year, I couldn't muster up enough strength to face my "friends" for the remaining weeks of inevitable encounters. At my mom's insistence, I came home to regroup for a bit.

My mom, who was at least as emotional as I was, picked me up at the Vancouver airport. Surprising my friends with my visit was fun—that kind of unplanned opportunity doesn't present itself too often.

But my younger brother Bryn's reaction to my unplanned visit was a sharp awakening.

While I had been working through my unhappiness in Wyoming, my Mom, Dad and Bryn had been working through their own challenges—challenges I had been oblivious to. Bryn had lost one of his kidneys to cancer when he was 11 months old, and in the past few months the function in his remaining kidney was declining after 16 years of wear and tear.

When he came upstairs to see me standing in the kitchen, his face turned that pale yellowish color common to people who are sick to their stomach.

"Mom? What's going on?" My mom instantly knew what he was thinking. "Megan's just come home for the week to regroup, Sweets. She wanted to surprise you. Nothing's wrong."

I felt guilty for surprising him. And as he wrapped his muscly, water-weight heavy arms around me, I realized the stress he was under—and that I had been oblivious to.

It didn't take long for Mom, Dad, Bryn and I to get used to being around each other again. When we were all together, it was as if we could lean on one another so the weight we were each carrying could be better distributed.

For the rest of the week, I held on tight to my mom and her rescue efforts. She insisted on treating me to a haircut: "Get something fresh and new, it will help you feel good!" So I did. (Let's just say, I gave Mötley Crüe a run for their money.) In keeping with the theory that it takes a village to raise a child, there was an impromptu tequila-sushi party with all the neighbors, "just because you're home!" There was a little bit of casual tennis. And then there was Chad.

Two days before heading back to Wyoming, I spent my entire day at Blue Mountain Racquet Club, my tennis home away from home.

Occasionally, the club would host open houses, with racquet demos, games and serving competitions. On this particular Saturday, I looked forward to the serving competition so that I could show off my fresh-off-the-college-court skill. I was with two of the coaches in their office, sitting on the desk with my feet up, making wisecracks, when an unfamiliar silhouette appeared in the doorway.

"Hey, guys." Seeing his motorcycle helmet under one arm and tennis bag hanging by his side, I felt something in my chest lurch as I recognized him.

Swinging my feet off the desk, I didn't stop to think before I spoke. "Chad Warren, you're alive!"

He looked exactly as I remembered him three years earlier; maybe a little healthier. Broad shoulders, sun-bronzed skin, and those unforgettable soft brown eyes... all that tall, dark and handsome stuff.

Understandably caught off guard, he half-chuckled, and said, "Yes, I am."

I didn't bother excusing myself from the conversation with my friends to escort Chad to the courts. Skipping alongside, I asked, "So what happened to you? I heard you were sick."

"I was. Very sick, but what the doctors did seemed to work, so now I'm just trying to get healthy again and get back into tennis." He recited it as though he'd answered the same question many times before.

When it was my turn in the serving competition, I stepped up to the baseline and cranked a few over the net. My best clocked 98 miles per hour. I had never done that in my life!

Impressed with myself, I spun around to make sure that Chad was equally impressed with what he had just witnessed. He was, and gave the reaction I hoped for—eyebrows up, validating head nod. "That's pretty good. Can you do that again?"

"Uh, yeah." I totally could.

Uh, no. I totally could not. I cranked out a few more at 90 mph, even one at 100 mph, but none of them were even close to being in the service box. I didn't care. Whatever. No big deal. I totally didn't care.

Once the afternoon's activities were over, Chad made it clear that, even though my serves weren't worth staying around for, he was willing to continue our conversation. "What's your number? A few friends are going out tonight. I'll give you a call."

I didn't think to save the number he left on my voicemail. I just hoped that when I was back from Wyoming, we'd run in to each other again. I could wait two months.

TATTOOS?!?

It was the summer of 2005, and when I landed back in Vancouver, I had only one plan—to rediscover happiness and confidence somewhere between the walls of my parents' home and running the seawalls that surrounded the city.

Home from Wyoming for good, unsure of what would be next for me as a student or a tennis player, I gravitated to the place I was most comfortable: the tennis club. The summer would be deliberately carefree, working at the sport I once loved, surrounded by friends I'd always loved.

The first tournament of the summer season was the New Westminster Open. I showed up one evening in time to watch a fellow coach being punished by a guy in a white tank top that showcased the tattoos wrapped around his muscles. I sat down on a spectators' bench beside my friend Todd and asked, "Who is Max playing?"

"Chad Warren."

It was a surprise. I didn't know Chad was good enough to be play at the Open level, and I also couldn't believe he was beating Max, one of the best players I knew. It was rare to see Max scream and sneeze around the court like Monica Seles. But all that came out of my mouth was: "Chad has tattoos?"

"You like that, do you? Someone's got a crush on Chad." Shut it, Todd. You don't know what you're talking about. That would be weird.

Chad won the match. I didn't stay to talk to either of them. I wanted to, but Chad looked really tired, and I figured if he continued to play the summer tournaments, I'd likely see him soon.

I PUSHED MYSELF TOO HARD.

I'll start by saying that my parents are alive and well. We almost lost my mother at one point, but she fought hard. She hasn't had a smooth ride, and had a nasty lung infection similar to tuberculosis. But after a year of heavy antibiotics, her health began to come back so she can enjoy life.

She walks every day and plays bridge often. According to my Aunty Pat, who she often plays with, she is quite a good bridge player. Mom is on treatment called Revlimid for her multiple myeloma, and has had good results despite the side effects. I'm very impressed and proud—maybe the best word is inspired. She seems truly happy, maybe the happiest I've ever known her to be.

As for my dad, he gets checked every six months and that remaining kidney is working hard. He hikes whenever he can and still plays squash once or twice a week. I'm really baffled by my father—he has had so much to deal with and he does so much for my mother. He is in his final year of work before retiring and I know he can't be done soon enough.

But I'm so proud of him, and happy he found this career 16 years ago. He is revered all over Canada for his work in the non-profit sector, and I know he'll continue in some capacity after retirement. I have even considering a move into fundraising myself.

My father is a private man, and I hope that he is holding up okay with all that is happening around him. He is very strong—I'm not sure they make them any stronger!

He is my mentor and confidante, but I can be so stubborn and distant with both of my parents. I love them very much and they have been nothing but supportive and caring for my entire life.

I didn't get much remission. About two or three years. I used that time to get in shape, and even attempted a comeback on the local tennis scene. I had never been so focused. I was a man on a mission.

Unfortunately the comeback was short lived, as my body couldn't handle what I was throwing at it. I suppose the combination of the bone-marrow transplant, the chemo and radiation, and the anti-rejection drugs I was taking at the time weren't benefiting my fitness level.

At any rate, I entered my first tournament in over five years, the New Westminster Open, and the first event of the 2005 summer series, a local men's open circuit.

Because I had been away from tennis for so long, I had to play the qualifying matches to earn my way into the main draw. I was playing some shaky tennis, but I managed to get through.

My last qualifying match was one I won't forget. I played someone I shouldn't have had any problem with but, of course, I put so much pressure on myself that I ended up dropping a set and grinding out a third set. I pushed on and won the third set. I pushed on and won the match but then the trouble began.

I ate apples and drank a sports drink, but nothing was going to stop the inevitable. I began to panic, and warned the tournament organizers that I was in trouble and might need an ambulance. Sure enough, I started to cramp everywhere. I was going into shock.

All I wanted to do that afternoon was enjoy my victory by cruising around on my motorcycle.

But I had really done it. I pushed myself too hard and there I was, being taken away in an ambulance.

I never really found out what happened to me that day. I spent four or five hours in the hospital and was released.

I was never the same after that day, but four days later I was scheduled to play my first round in the Open. I promised myself that I would take it very easy out there. I ended up winning the first set easily (6-2) only to let the second go (0-6). I went up in the third 4-2 (30-0) only to run out of steam. That was it for my singles comeback.

THE START OF MEGAN
AND CHAD

The second tournament of the summer circuit was at Blue Mountain, where I had home court advantage. I was watching my small-time ex-boyfriend get badly beaten when Chad sauntered up next to me in the viewing gallery.

He seemed genuinely disgusted when I explained that we had dated the summer before. "Ew, Meg. Really? You went out with him!"

"I know, I know. He wasn't that bad, really." I don't know why I said that, because he was that bad. Why was I defending myself to Chad anyway? "What about you? Do you have a lady in your life?" He, far less uncomfortable with addressing the topic than I, explained he had been in a serious relationship with a girl named Katharine when he was sick. It had been awhile since they had broken up, but he made it very clear what good friends they continued to be.

Inevitably, the "ex" conversation came to a halt, followed by 30 seconds of silence, before I spat out what I'd really been thinking about.

"So what kind of cancer did you have? What happened to you?" There really wasn't any subtle way to ask someone "Wut up with yo' cancer?" so I just asked and hoped I wasn't about to enhance our already awkward silence.

"Well, you don't hold back do you?"

I couldn't tell if he was amused or annoyed.

"Sorry."

"No, nothing to be sorry about! It's just that people don't normally ask because they think it will make me uncomfortable. But it's more uncomfortable when people tiptoe around the conversation, trying to find out the details without ever asking what is really on their minds."

Oh thank goodness. I exhaled all at once: "I just thought, you seem healthy now, so it would be ok to ask, and if you didn't want to talk about it you would just say that."

"I had multiple myeloma. It's a rare blood cancer. Apparently I'm one of the youngest people in North America to have been diagnosed with it. I had to go through a whole whack of radiation, chemo, steroids and then I had a bone marrow transplant."

A bone marrow transplant. I could only guess at how to spell "marrow," never mind understand what a bone marrow transplant entailed. But I nodded and made sympathetic noises, and put words together that I hoped might indicate I knew what he was talking about. "Ah yes, aha, I see, oh geez, that sounds rough, gotcha."

Watching the ball go from side to side on the courts below, he said, "The transplant seemed to take, and I've just spent the last year trying to build up my body again. It's been a doozy but I'm feeling good now." He hadn't made eye contact throughout the conversation, but now he looked at me.

"That's crazy, Chad. I don't know what to say." I had never talked to anyone about cancer before, but I had a feeling that the conversation was an unusual experience for both of us. He talked about it in the same way I had wanted him to tell me about it: simply and honestly

"Thanks for telling me." Really, thank you.

We continued to stand quietly next to one another. I felt that what he had confided in me deserved a little bit of silence.

I don't know how long we were there, but this time the silence was not awkward.

Chad was the first one to speak this time. "We're looking for coaches for this summer up at Hollyburn. If you're looking for work, I could talk to Rufus, the head pro, and see if you can come in for an interview."

I replied in one breath. "I am, and I'd love that. Thank you. Does that mean I'd be working with you?"

"Yes. So you better not think you're going to get away with any of your slacking off college crap." He was teasing and I loooooooved it.

"What? Please. Slack? Me? Never." "Okay, good. Give me a call, or send me an email at work. I'll talk to you soon, you little shit disturber." He made his departure. "Enjoy watching your boyfriend play."

That conversation was the start of Megan and Chad.

A few days later, I bounced up to Chad as he and his friend watched the doubles final, and said, "Hi, boyfriend!"

I relished the frequent Chad encounters the tournaments provided. My confidence had revived since I'd come home from cowtown, and I was comfortable in the friendliness between us.

Clearly taken aback, Chad did a half-turn to look at me, "Excuse me?"

"I said, hi, boyfriend. Didn't you hear me?"

"Hi, I'm Megan." I leaned across Chad to extend my hand in introduction to his friend, Andrew. "Anyways, I just thought I'd come over and say hi. Enjoy the match. Bye!"

I AM TOTALLY HALF
BIKER CHICK.

I started my first real coaching job at Hollyburn Country Club's summer tennis camps after Chad set up the interview. He wasn't there for my first week of work, so it gave me a chance to settle in without being too distracted with maintaining my man-friendship. By the time he called the following Sunday, I'd almost lost track of how long he'd been away.

"Hey! Back already?" I chirped.

"How was your week? Didn't slack off without me there, did you?"

I ignored that. "How was your trip?" As social as Chad seemed, I wondered what it was about the Lone Ranger road trip to the prairies that interested him.

As he spoke, I tried to imagine him riding through the prairies. "It's nice to get out on the road and see family, but I started to get tired on the way back. That's a long time to stay focused on a bike, sitting in that position."

I wanted him to keep talking. He was a good storyteller, but he promptly turned the conversation away from himself. "So, what are you doing today? Want to see a movie later?"

"Um, sure. I'm playing tennis with my dad, but after that could work." I was caught off guard, not expecting this friendship to extend off-court so quickly.

"Okay, it's my dad's birthday, so I'm going to go play with him as well. I can come pick you up after, and we can go for dinner before the movie." Blindsiding me with dinner...not this cowboy's first rodeo.

"You can't pick me up at my parents house on your bike. It will freak them out. I can just meet you there." As the words came out of my mouth, I wished I had a pacifier to shut me up. I sounded like such a baby.

"...But I've never been on a motorcycle before, so let's meet a little earlier and you can still take me for a spin."

Pleased, he arranged a plan. "Deal. I'll bring an extra helmet. Meet you at 5:15?"

"See you there." Somewhat confused about why he'd give up his Sunday night and drive 30 minutes to see a movie with me, I was excited nonetheless.

I was transferring my favorite ripped Abercrombie jeans from the washing machine to the dryer when my Mom walked by. "You're not going to go out with another tennis guy are you?"

I turned my head slightly so she could hear me but could not make eye contact. "No! No. I'm not going out with another tennis guy. We're just friends."

"Okay." She sounded like she took my word for it, but her question made me think: Was this a date? It's totally not a date. Chad's a grownup. I'm way younger than he is. I'd be a fool if I considered this a date.

When I arrived at our non-date, I barely recognized Chad in non-sports clothes, leaning up against his bike, one helmet on the bike, the other in his hand. With the sun setting in the background, he greeted me with a cowboy sexy smile.

"So this is it, huh?"

"This is it," he said. "Ready?"

"I guess so. No wheelies or anything though right? My parents are expecting me to come home tonight. Alive." I said as cutely as possible, trying to hide any nerves while he clipped me into his heavy passenger helmet.

Feeling a bit like a dashboard bobble head, I fished for a compliment, "So how good do I look right now?"

"You look good. Now get on, relax, and hold on to me."

I can do that.

Chad revved the gears, making that obnoxious, loud engine noise bikes make as they warm up. I liked it, but my clammy hands reminded me that I was way out of my comfort zone.

As we merged on the highway, he shifted into higher gears. I love it I love it I love it! I felt *so* cool. Chad lifted his wrist in a half wave, acknowledging any other bikers we passed by.

I yelled from behind, "Do you know them?"

He slowed down to hear me over the wind and engine. "*What?* I can't hear you when we're riding."

I shouted back, "I asked, do you know them?"

Without making me feel like an idiot, he answered "No, just one biker acknowledging another."

"Oh, okay. Cool!" I knew that. I am totally half biker chick.

I was too nervous to release either of my hands from Chad's waist to wave at the next biker, so I nodded my big bobble head in their direction. If this was a cool club, I was pleased to act as an honorary member for the night.

Chad yelled back to me, "We'll do one more exit on the highway and turn around, okay?"

I yelled back. "*Okaaayy*!!"

He ripped on the gears and as we tore up the highway, I lifted myself up enough to peer over his shoulder to see how fast we were going. 200 kilometers per hour.

"How you doing?" he asked, patting me on the thigh.

"Fine. I'm good. 200 kilometers! That's crazy, Chad!" I couldn't hear him, but I could see he was chuckling as we whipped back in the direction we came.

That's when I realized I had been holding on to his waist for the last 20 minutes without once thinking to feel what kind of muscle he was working with under his green cotton long-sleeve.

I pulled a little closer. It was rock hard. Tight and packed with solid muscle. Chaddd, how did I not notice this before??!

I was totally and certainly attracted to my man-friend. And once I realized that, I couldn't un-know it.

The friendship of Chad and Megan had just changed gears.

SO, HOW MANY BOYFRIENDS DID YOU LEAVE DOWN THERE?

We pulled back into the restaurant parking lot at the same speed we'd left it. I was relieved it was over, but sad I had no further excuse to keep my arms wrapped around him.

I awkwardly shimmied myself off the bike and tried to unclip my helmet. Chad reached over to help me before I reenacted a shampoo ad, shaking my blonde locks from the constraints of the helmet.

"Cute." He observed. "You did good. Did you like it?"

"You said you wouldn't go fast!" I smacked his shoulder. "Don't think I didn't see the speedometer go past 200 kilometers! But yes, I liked it." I was quickly realizing how slowly I wanted this night to pass.

"Okay, good. Let's eat," he said, neatly tucking the helmets away.

As we walked through the restaurant lounge, I was positive everyone knew I had just been on a motorcycle and, as a result, thought I was so cool.

I pulled myself into the booth and Chad took the seat across from me. This was the first time the two of us had spent time together without the distractions of work or tennis.

I hadn't even thought of anything to talk about!

Thankfully, I didn't need to. Talking with Chad felt like picking up in the middle of a conversation we had never started nor ended.

He asked what happened at Wyoming that made me leave; and to my own surprise, I answered more honestly that I normally would with someone I was just getting to know.

He asked more questions and seeming to understand why I had made the decisions I had. He offered stories about his experience playing tennis for South Eastern Louisiana and his similar struggles with his college coach.

To others, I typically talked about leaving Wyoming with a deliberate shallowness, but with Chad I felt comfortable being truthful about my unhappiness there and my determination to reclaim my game at another school. I wasn't sure why I chose to be so honest with him, especially since we didn't know each other that well, but he seemed to know how I felt.

After giving me a look that reassured me what I had shared with him was safe, I appreciated it when he lightened the conversation.

"So how many boyfriends did you leave down there?"

"Excuse me? I didn't leave any boyfriends down there." Honestly.

"I know you've got a few in your back pocket. A cute girl like you? Whether you know it or not, and I think you do."

"No. You're wrong," I answered, trying to be as humble as possible.

"Oh please, Meg. You know you're cute. And even if you're not a flirt, you're friendly—and you know there are at least…"

(he paused) "…five guys interpreting your friendliness for flirting—never knowing that they don't actually stand a chance."

How did he draw this conclusion? I had never given much thought to my guy-friends and here is this old guy, laying it out for me!

I lowered my eyes to my drink. "Enough about me. I'm sure you've got plenty of lady groupies following you around." I only wanted to be right so that I could find out more about what kind of girls he was interested in. But before he could answer, the waitress slipped the bill on our table and we both reached for our wallets.

"No. Put your money away." From the irritation in his tone, you'd think I'd just asked for the last bite of his steak fajita.

"No. Please take my money. My treat. You can get the movie."

He handed his credit card to the waitress, who had been standing off to the side, pretending not to listen. "At least let me feel like a man, would you?"

I retreated with a simple, "Thank you."

"You're welcome. And don't even think about getting the movie either," he pronounced as he stood up and waited for me to walk in front of him.

It was the first time I'd been with a guy whose decisiveness and good manners made me feel taken care of.

I felt special, smart and pretty, three markers of confidence I had lost in my final Wyoming semester. As we walked across the street to the movie theatres, I squinted into the light of the setting sun to look at the tall, tanned man walking beside me. Another lost feeling resurfaced—I was happy. Very happy.

Requiring no compromise, we decided on the 7:20p.m. showing of Spider-Man. Between my heaping spoonfuls of frozen yogurt and his popcorn and Sour Patch Kids, it felt like we hadn't stopped talking since getting off his bike two hours earlier. As the theatre dimmed, I propped my feet up on the back of the chair in front of me, unintentionally causing the rip on the thigh of my jeans to stretch open. This became an invitation for Chad's right hand.

He reached over and gave the three-centimeter area of exposed skin a light stroke. "Hmmmm...soft," he said without diverting his eyes from the screen.

I don't know what was more of a relief: that he hadn't made eye contact when he said that, or that I had remembered to shave my legs.

"Chad! Get out of there!" I swatted his hand away, pretending to be appalled at his forwardness.

"And for the record, they're always this soft." Flirting!

As the trailers lit up the theatre, we whispered "I'd see that" and "I'll wait for the rental" reviews to each other. With all the leaning in, I forgot what movie we were there to see.

You are in a movie theatre. You are here to watch a movie. It's called Spider-Man. Pull yourself together. I smiled at him as I straightened my posture until our shoulders no longer touched. As exciting, yet comfortable, this evening had been, I wanted to be sure I wasn't misreading this new companionship.

The movie felt long. Following the plot became increasingly difficult as I tried not to think about our touching knees, wondering if it was as intentional on his part as it was on mine. Was I the only one noticing our forearms and hands brushing against one another as we reached in for popcorn?

After the movie, we stood by his two-wheeled chariot, neither one of us rushing to say goodbye. Chad gave me a big bear hug before popping on his helmet and swinging his leg up over the saddle of his bike. "That was fun, little one. See you tomorrow, bright and early?"

"That was fun. See you tomorrow."

On his bike, he was at eye level to me. I held the sides of his helmet in my hands, pulled him close and kissed him where the plastic covered his mouth.

Letting his helmet go and slowly pulling away, I smiled as though we had done that a thousand times. "Bye, Chad."

Whether he felt the same or not, this non-date dinner and a movie had changed my entire summer.

TENNIS HELPED BRING ME BACK TO LIFE.

Tennis has played a huge role in my life. It's given me some of my closest friends, paid for my university, given me work, not to mention so many memories. And most importantly, it gave me Megan.

My favorite childhood memories are of summers spent at the Lethbridge Tennis Club, a small six-court facility right down the alley from my house. The club was set across from Henderson Lake and in behind the baseball stadium that was the home of our LA (Lethbridge, Alberta) Dodgers—it was a beautiful setting. I'd get there early in the morning to play with the seniors and be there sometimes past midnight, playing late night games under the lights with the club pro and his friends. I did that from the age of 10 until I moved to Vancouver at 15... so much freedom. I can remember my mother screaming at me from across the park to come home for lunch—or bed, depending on the time of day.

When I arrived in Vancouver, it wasn't long before I began to pal around with the other guys in my age group playing the local junior circuit. A group of us became close friends and travelled to all the tournaments together, terrorizing the streets from here to

Montreal. We all went on to get scholarships to play in the States. We stay in touch, but everyone is spread out around the world: Jesse in Louisiana, James C in Montreal, James G in New York, Justin in Australia. I'm really proud of these guys and I miss not having them around.

University was a whole new experience, and I savored every moment of it. I'd taken a year off after high school to write my SATs and apply to universities. There are so many choices in the U.S. and I was down to talking to two or three, so I looked on the map and picked the furthest one from home, where I knew it would be warm.

This is where my dislike for tennis began—somewhere in that year off, I lost my confidence on the court, and it didn't help that the coach I had signed with quit a week before school started. I wasn't happy with my on-court performance throughout college, but I loved practicing in the sun, and we had a blast traveling all over the southern states.

I certainly enjoyed the benefits of being a student athlete in the states, and exploited it to the maximum. I have many close friends from university and have reunited with my teammates over the years even though most of them now live back in their native lands. We had guys from Sweden, Argentina, France, Holland and two from Canada.

My friend Jesse joined me at university my second year, and it was really cool to have a close friend share that experience. He really helped me to stay on track with tennis and school. Jesse ended up staying down there to do his master's degree and married a sweet southern belle—they now have two beautiful girls.

Since being diagnosed, tennis has helped bring me back to life. It makes me feel like a better person. I began taking coaching more seriously and was the 2003/2004 U18 B.C. Indoor Nationals squad coach. I took our team to Toronto to compete both those years. It felt strange thinking about the fact that I was one of those kids only 10 years earlier. They were far better behaved than our group, and at least waited until they were out of the tournament before hitting up the beers…little bastards.

FOR TWO?

"Dinner tonight? I feel like Thai, do you like Thai?" I don't know if it was his voice I enjoyed hearing so much or if it was the words "dinner" and "tonight" that made the sides of my mouth turn up. Though I saw Chad every day at work, I had grown impatient waiting for the opportunity to get together off-court again.

"Come to mine at 6:30 tonight. You can park in my visitor parking lot. I've got my Mom's car so I'll drive us to a place near here. It's the best Thai food on the North Shore." Decisiveness - I love it.

Non-date/date, commence! My white pants, brown tube top and gold chunky earrings were ready to go. Then, the parental border guards: Brenda and Tony. Yes, I am going out with Chad. No, I won't be back tonight; I'll be staying out at Michelle's. Yes, I'll be home tomorrow morning with the car. Parentals puhlleaasse, I've got to get this perfect show on the road!

My wavy sun-streaked hair had air-dried perfectly by the time I pulled up to Chad's building. *I look as good as I feel*, I told myself. Calm and cool, I also reminded myself that Chad and I were just friends.

I was nervous-excited. My underarms were damper than any girl would like them to be when showing up at a boy's house, so I hurriedly fanned them in the elevator.

I knocked on his door and looked away, so as to not look like a crazy lady eyeballing him through the peephole. His hair was freshly buzzed, showing off the small peaks of his newly receding hairline. Compared to the groomed, accessorized guys from college, Chad's no-maintenance style wasn't one I was familiar with, but I decided this must be what real men looked like.

"Well, don't you look all summery!" He observed upon swinging the door inward. Two steps into the hallway, and his arms wrapped around me in a body-relaxing hug.

He let go to give me the 20-second tour of his studio apartment. A blanket was folded perfectly over the arm of one couch, while the other had a throw pillow that complimented the neutral palette, demonstrating the care this bachelor put into his home.

We left for the restaurant. Although I didn't know when, I was confident I'd be back in the bachelor pad sometime soon.

He held the door for me as I stepped in to the restaurant's empty waiting area, taking in the aroma of warm sauce and rice.

If tacky decor made this place "the best Thai food on the North Shore" then Chad was bang-on with his review. The big Buddha statues holding dollar store mints while guarding the trickling waterfall were admittedly cheerful.

A woman who spoke heavily Thai-accented English held two fingers up. "For two?"

"Yes, please." Chad confirmed politely. We followed her to a table by the window where she barely waited for us to sit before she slapped the plastic menu-novels on the table and walked away.

"So, what do you normally have here?" I asked as I opened the sticky menu.

"Normally I get the chicken, but I think we should do one of the meals for two." He pointed to the photograph on the menu.

I got more comfortable in my chair as I concluded that he was unlikely to order a meal for two with any of his buddies. All signs were pointing to date status.

Our table had a view of the ocean, and the setting sun coming through the windows was warm. While we sipped our pineapple juice cocktails and dunked our chicken skewers in peanut sauce (which I was positive was just melted peanut butter) there was finally a break in conversation that allowed me to ask about the women in his life.

"What kind of girls do you go out with, Chad Warren?"

"Ahhhh…well…" He shifted in his chair.

I was so keen to hear what he was going to say that I interrupted to help the answer along. "Blondes? Brunettes? Sporty types? Not so sporty types?" I was hoping he would say sandy blonde hair, just like mine, and sporty, just like me.

"My girlfriends in college were all really sporty. A few were actually kind of like you."

Yesssss!!

"They were good athletes, spunky, cute. But now they're all a bit different. I guess I might have a thing for blondes, but I don't discriminate." He was handsome, even when he smirked.

"Neither do I." I dunked my last bite of chicken into the peanut butter.

"Oh, yeah? Well, if the guy you were watching play at the Blue Mountain Tournament is any indication of what kind of guys you go out with—you need to start picking better guys. Knowing that you went out with him is almost a deal breaker."

He went on to outline that he had recently dated a girl from his building who was a nurse, and another friend of a friend—but both had conveniently ended in the last few weeks.

The bill came, and I offered to pay, but once again he reached for the bill and slid his credit card inside. "I try to put $1,000 on my credit card each month." It made no sense to me, but it sounded calculated, the kind of thing grownups say.

As we sat in the car deciding how to extend the evening past dinner, I offered, "I'm staying over at Michelle's house tonight. Do you want to come hang out there for awhile?"

"Sure."

I wondered what Michelle would think of me showing up with a guy who was nearly a decade older than anyone I had spent time with before.

She wasn't fazed in the slightest. Time skipped from 10:00 p.m. to after midnight in what felt like 20 minutes before Chad politely excused himself, "so you can have your girl time."

Standing beside his car in the balmy summer night air, he embraced me again. "Goodnight, princess."

"Night, Chad. Chat to you tomorrow perhaps?"

"Sure thing." He ducked into his car and backed out of the steep driveway.

"So have you kissed yet?" Between rolling up chip bags and putting fruit back into the fridge, Michelle caught me off guard. Even with that innocent kiss on the helmet last week, I had not thought about it. "No! He's too old, don't you think?"

"No. He's good-looking. That shaved head. Meggie—yes. Totally."

Well, when you put it that way...

I drifted off to sleep that night imaging if or when I might have the opportunity to kiss my man-friend.

WANT TO GO FOR A WALK?

Evidently the feeling was mutual. Dinner plans were made for the following night.

Despite my best efforts to convince Mom and Dad (i.e, the car owners) that I needed the car for another night, they wouldn't budge.

"Since you'll be staying at Michelle's, why don't you get her to pick you up?" Dad challenged the logistics of my plans.

Didn't they have *any* idea what it's like to be 20!?!?! Of course they did. That's why they were trying to slow me down.

Michelle agreed to drive me to work first thing in the morning, and I tried to be a big girl about spending nearly three hours of coaching wages on the cab ride from my parent's house to the North Shore where dinner with Chad would validate the wisdom of my investment.

Pulling up to the front, I tried my best to ignore the $50 fare and get out of the cab as collected as possible.

"Com'n up." He muffled through the intercom.

I waited for the elevator, taking a careful look in the lobby mirror. Straightened hair, my goes-with-everything black Bebe skirt and pale pink tank top—I was pleased with my reflection despite the hair-frizzing effects of the cab's humidity.

Here we go, date number two. (Or was it three?)

Thank goodness his door wasn't locked or the momentum of opening it to let myself in would have slammed me right into a closed door.

"So you just walk in now do you?" Chad's voice came from around the corner.

"Yep. It was open." I dumped my bag in the hallway.

"Are you staying over or something? What's the bag for?"

I explained my plans to stay at Michelle's place and go to work from there in the morning.

"Oh." I may have detected disappointment in his voice.

Hands hardly relaxed by my sides, I stood staring up at Chad, in jeans and a navy "Country Clubs - Not For Everyone" t-shirt. I didn't wait more than three seconds before I got the hug I was waiting for.

Awesome.

To avoid an awkward long-hold, I let go and strolled over to the couch where I laid like Cleopatra across his big, obviously well-used cushions. "I'm ready when you are." Rephrase that. "I mean, for dinner." So much for not being awkward. I smiled at him over the back of the couch.

"Let's go. We can come back here to get your bag after dinner and I'll drive you to Michelle's."

At dinner, it was clear the dynamic between us had shifted. Our conversation was more or less the same, but our eyes were having an entirely different conversation. Chemistry confirmed. There was no denying it any longer.

"Want to go for a walk?" Chad asked as he wiped his mouth and signed the bill. "Ambleside is a nice beach, we can walk there."

He didn't suggest this walk as negotiable, and I was quite happy to oblige.

When we got to his car, Chad opened the door for me. As I lowered myself into the seat, I could feel his body heat close behind me. Consequently, my body temperature also rose as he closed the door and walked to the driver's side.

He ducked into the car, looked at me (I was desperately trying not to make eye contact), and gently touched his hand to my thigh. "Smooth again!"

If he wasn't so lovely, he might seem like a bit of a pervert.

I let my body lean in toward his side of the car. Each time he shifted between third and fourth gear, the top of his knuckles brushed my thigh.

Seemingly focused on the road, we sat quietly, with only one focus; third gear, shift. Fourth gear, shift down. Third gear, shift.

A few blocks from the beach he moved his hand to rest on my thigh. His hand was soft and far less clammy than mine. It took me another block before I rested my left hand on top of his, knitting my fingers between his.

Chad parked the car so we were facing the cloudy sunset over the ocean. It was going to be a movie-perfect kiss and this is where I would make it happen.

The backs of our hands brushed against one another as we walked along the sand-dusted pavement towards the beach. Finally, he softly took my hand and held it.

We walked towards a statue overlooking the water. Yeah, it's spectacular, I know, I know. I'll appreciate it later. I'm busy planning my man-friend kiss.

We got to the end of the pier. Without letting go of his hand, I turned to face him.

But the sight of his kind brown eyes gazing down at me caused my confidence to disappear.

And instead of staging the next great first kiss of all time, I started yammering on about something meaningless before I finally interrupted myself and leaned towards him.

With one hand holding mine, he reached for my waist with the other to pull me closer, then leaned in for a kiss. I stepped closer, allowing it to continue. Yes. Almost perfect.

Too much tongue?! Or are my lips too pursed, like a grandma with no teeth? This is not awesome.

When we finally pulled away from our frog-grandma smooch, I came out with, "It was movie perfect."

Jesus, it doesn't get any more G-rated Disney princess than that.

Thankfully, he chuckled. "Is that right?" He took my hand more confidently as we walked back to the car.

"If you can't get ahold of Michelle, it's fine if you'd like to stay at mine," he said. "I'll drive us to work in the morning."

As though she had some spidey-sense, Michelle didn't pick up her phone, leaving me no choice but to stay the night at Chad's.

The silence in the car confirmed that neither of us was prepared to discuss what was happening, but the energy between us was overwhelming.

We stepped into the elevator like anxious teenagers waiting for their parents to leave so they can have the house to themselves. The doors were inches from closing when Chad pulled me against him and kissed me deeply.

By the ninth floor, his hands had made their way down my low back and over my skirt. The doors opened on his floor to reveal a couple waiting to get on, and like teenagers, we halted. Chad acknowledged his neighbors before we continued down the hall.

We hurried through his door, rushing as though we needed to make up for the 20 seconds we had just missed.

The moment we were through the door, he kissed me again, walking me backwards towards his bed.

After I flopped gracelessly backward on the bed, he kicked off his flip-flops and kissed his way up over my clothed body. His lips met mine and I reached under his shirt, reacquainting myself with the muscles I had felt when holding him on his bike.

Bless and curse the male body for being capable of such a wonderful, tight torso. I pulled his shirt over his head to reveal the tanned, muscular body leaning over me.

All focus and control had been lost. Within seconds of his shirt coming off, mine was off, and he was kissing his way back down my stomach towards my inner thighs.

Megan this isn't you! What are you doing? You don't do this!

Holding both sides of his face, I pulled him up to kiss me.

Conscience vs. chemistry—this would be the first time in my young adult life that I allowed chemistry to win. Before my conscience was able to rebut, Chad was on top of me, my legs wrapped around him, encouraging him further.

I knew I could stop, but I was too intrigued by how natural it felt being together like this.

As we moved together, he held my hands cinematically above my head.

This was by far the most unexpected, memorable, exciting night of my young romantic life.

The next day, when my mom asked where I'd slept, I said, "Chad's couch." I didn't feel good about lying, but I also didn't feel good about revealing that I am the kind of girl who sleeps in the bed of friends who are boys. Even those I might be totally and deeply attracted to, and who, when I wake up next to them, make me feel like I had been there a thousand mornings before.

I continued with the misleading statements (lies) about where I was sleeping over the next few weeks of summer. And even though my parents knew the answer, they still asked every night I wasn't at home. I was at Chad's. Or at my friend Adrienne's, and Jesse's. And then Chad's.

What Chad and I had felt significant. It didn't feel fleeting or fling-like, even though our age difference and the realization that I had still not graduated university were very polarizing at times. Chad and I were in a comfortable grey area between relationship and "just having fun."

We were simply serious about having fun.

CHAD NEEDS TO GET AWAY.

A little over a month after our first sleepover, our carefree summer together took a sharp turn toward reality. We had just walked out of the Granville Street Cinemas and were strolling streets bright with neon lights and the sounds of Thursday night bar-stars. I was used to him giving me his undivided attention when we were together, but tonight his mind was elsewhere.

"Do you want to go away with me this weekend?" he asked.

"Yeah, sure." I had never been on a weekend away. How very adult! "Where did you have in mind?"

"Anywhere. I just want to get out of here, away from everything for a few days," he replied, his face lit by the flashing signs.

"Is everything okay? You seem a little off today," I pried.

"Nope. I'm all good," he lied.

I pried further, listing off as many options as I could: Family? Work? Health? Me? Us? "So, I've had a few doctor visits lately, and some results have come back. And…it's not great."

In the weeks leading up to his news, I had noticed that our dates involved more snuggling on his couch watching late-night Letterman and Leno with fewer outings.

He'd started asking if I minded coming over to his apartment, saying that he'd "had a long day." He'd mentioned that his "batteries don't recharge as quickly as I'd like them to."

I recognized early in our friendship-relationship that Chad's medical life was different than the rest of his life. The two were kept separate and only a few carefully chosen friends were close enough to know about the complexities of living two lives. I felt honored to be one of them.

I adopted his vagueness when responding to questions about why Chad didn't come out more often. I'd generalize, saying something about how, although he's recovered, he sometimes needs to rest longer; maybe throwing in a joke or two about how he's old and says I should have my fun without him. But I always made sure that any answers to questions about Chad's health status ended in victory: "And now he's on a few maintenance drugs, but everything is great."

Though that part about the maintenance drugs was true, after Thursday night's news, it was clear there was a lot more going on than just fatigue.

My parents weren't happy when I told them Chad and I would be going away for the weekend. Had I told them the real motive for getting away, they might have been more accepting of the idea, but I kept the details to myself, not wanting them to think Chad's health affected our relationship. Even though it sometimes did.

"Just to Harrison Hot Springs." Our destination wasn't more that 45 minutes out of town. "Chad's been needing to get away," was all I said.

The name alone, Harrison Hot Springs, gave my Dad reason to shoot protective glares at Chad as he lifted my bag into the trunk of his car.

On the car ride, our runs through the damp forest trails, and soaking in the allegedly healing hot springs, I learned more detail about the difficulties and side effects of Chad's cancer. He had discovered a few lumps in his chest and back, and on this mini-vacay I was told they were tumors—not fat deposits as he had originally explained to me. One of the many complications of an incurable cancer. With my growing knowledge of the disease, I was forced to recognize that as active and playful as Chad could be, there was no escaping the stress his body was under.

When we got back from Harrison, all the "stuff" about rising cancer counts and new drug protocols was out in the open. Our summer went on, but with an adapted normalcy. We had our first fights, first make-ups, first conversation about weddings, and our circle of mutual friends grew.

Chad and I had become such good companions that our honesty often caused us to stumble into "real relationship issues"—like the ongoing discussion about what school I would go to in January.

Though he was supportive and offered valuable advice, the more we talked about it, the harder it was to ignore it. I would eventually be leaving again.

It was a warm September Saturday when I got the deciding call from the tennis coach at Jacksonville University in Florida. "We'd like to offer you a full-ride scholarship." I called Chad right after accepting the offer, and his enthusiasm was genuine.

I knew I was leaving soon; he knew I was leaving soon, and I knew that changed our light-hearted serious relationship. But I wanted him to be my boyfriend. Because somehow that title acknowledged his significance in my life.

July, August, September, now October...why wasn't I his girlfriend yet?!

When I asked, his response was the obvious: "You're young, man. I can't have a girlfriend in college. I've been there; I know what it's like. You don't need me at home holding you down."

That was an explanation I had heard in various forms throughout the fall. I took his comments about me being young and needing to experience college for myself as insults, and rebutted every time.

Then we started the what-are-we-doing cycle. Every three weeks we would give each other up for a week on the grounds of, "if this isn't going anywhere, then what's the point?" There would be a week of stubbornness; then one of us would send a text message.

"You sure are a stubborn little smartass, aren't you, Meggles?"

As though he'd been gone for years, I'd respond with the longing I felt for him, with my need to hear from him.

"Well, well. Look at who misses me."

"Maybe. Movie?"

"Sure."

And we'd dance again.

NASTY FUCKING DRUG

I began a new treatment after finding several tumors growing in me that were originally misdiagnosed as fat deposits. I felt two in the left side of my chest. There was also one on my upper back and another, the ding-donger, pressing on a nerve on my spinal cord. The pain from the pressure on my spinal cord sent me to the hospital after several nights without sleep.

They immediately put me on steroids, and the pain eased within the hour.

The treatment I began was Thalidomide, in combination with the steroid Dexamethesone. Nasty fucking drug gave me permanent neuropathy in my feet, nerve damage that makes it feel like my feet are permanently frozen.

One afternoon in November, my excitement and horror collided like thunderclouds when I realized why I was so desperate to have Chad as my boyfriend.

Jesus. I fucking love him.

That's what my problem has been!

What do you do when you have information like this? You can't just sit on it. Especially when Chad is the person I tell everything to.

And if you love someone, they deserve to know it right? Right? I mean, what kind of world would that be if we walked around not telling people things as wonderful as that they are loved?

I had to do it. Even while we were in our friend cycle, I wanted him to know.

After an evening of coaching, Chad and I walked out of the tennis club together. Tonight, I would say something.

Deep breath.

"So, I think I know why I've been so crazy around you lately." I won't turn back now. Out with it.

"I think I love you."

There. I've said it. Now you know.

"No, you don't."

Wait, what?

It took a few weeks of not seeing each other outside of coaching hours for us to get over the awkwardness of my confession and his loveless reaction. But come Christmas time, Chad and I resumed our casual, bafflingly honest relationship, just as before. Without any murmur of "I love you."

Chad hated Christmas. Even knowing that, I was surprised when he told me he was planning to skip it and spend the holiday in Mexico with a friend.

Without admitting to being disheartened, I drove them to the airport and hoped he would find a way to write me or at least acknowledge the care-package and card I handed him outside the departures drop-off.

My Chaddy,

In an effort to ignore your requests to make Christmas not happen, I figured—that would be too easy.

Having things to unwrap during the holidays is always fun—no matter what age you are. (Or pretend to be.)

Enjoy the sun and all its healing powers. I look forward to seeing you rested and relaxed—a feeling you deserve more than anyone.

You once casually mentioned to me that I make your life exciting. Thank you—but I should have kissed you and replied with, "Me too, and more than you know."

I'll miss you terribly over the holidays and whenever else I'm not with you.

Merry Christmas to the dearest man in my life.

Love, Megan xo
Mewwy Christmas

Date: 11:38am Tuesday, December 14, 2004
From: Chad
To: Megan
Subject: You are a very sweet little lady!

Thank you for the thoughtful care package. Lovin' the beaches. I hope you are having fun partying. I'm getting attacked by mosquitoes, so I have to go. Maybe could you pick us up from the airport? Talk to you soon. You would love it here. Chad

Date: 10:04pm Tuesday, December 14, 2004
From: Megan
To: Chad
Subject: Did you manage to escape Christmas?

Hope the bathroom cleaner and hand sanitizer comes in handy. What time does your flight arrive on the 26th?

I'm sure I would love it there, too – drink a shot of tequila for me (don't vomit like me though) ... and take a dip in the ocean for me, too, please.

Talk to you soon.

I'm so happy you are enjoying yourself.

Don't scratch your mosquito bites. Meggie xx

Date: 9:51am Wednesday, December 15, 2004
From: Chad
To: Megan
Subject: Re: did you manage to escape Christmas?

Hello Meggie,

Everything is great here, how are you? I am the reigning Connect Four champ. Undefeated. Meeting cool people from all over. I'll be in touch. Hope you are enjoying yourself. Bye for now. Chaddy

Date: 3:51pm Friday, December 17, 2004
From: Megan
To: Chad
Subject: I hope the little drummer boy trips

Chaderella,
I'm so happy to hear that your tanned ass is enjoying everything. I'm good, just finished my last day of work, so I'm going out with Monica and the ladies tonight...thought it necessary to consume some holiday bar-nog..... yippee!!
Talk to you soon...
booboobear
Have you set my picture up accordingly to face the water? Excellent. I'm glad to hear that.

Date: 3:53pm Sunday, December 19, 2004
From: Chad
To: Megan
Subject: Re: I hope the little drummer boy trips

I sense a different tone in your messages. Matty is still on the prowl, but having a good time. Some clouds in the days, but still getting some sun.

I'm feeling very relaxed...real life will be hard to get back to. Well, say hi to Moni and the ladies. Bye for now. Chaderella

Yes, your picture is enjoying the days in your absence. Very cute, by the way...love that ass!!!

Date: 1:15pm Monday, December 20, 2004
From: Megan
To: Chad
Subject: I ate frosty's nose

Chadilocks,

Glad to hear that Matty's exercising his game. Have you guys gone to see any of the glamorous Mexican-Romanian refugee dancers yet?

Monika and I (and whatever randoms we ran into) had a fab time out the other night... stumbled into bed at 5:30. So happy for you that you're relaxed. How does your body feel in the heat?

My dog says he wishes you could be at winter solstice....and he misses you.

Xo pookybear

What does this different tone sound like?

Date: 1:10pm Wednesday, December 22, 2004
From: Chad
To: Megan
Subject: Re: Don't Surf

I was in the water today, playing in the waves, and a school of eight-inch-long fish came at me, jumping through the waves. I had my one big drinking night last night, and I feel terrible. It was big for me, anyway. Anyway, hope you're relaxing and preparing for your new adventure. Chaderella (what the fuck is that)

Date: 7:41pm Wednesday, December 22, 2004
From: Megan
To: Chad
Subject: I tipped over the manger...

Chadillena,

I'm sorry that you don't feel good after your run-in with Mr. Quervo. I had a run-in last night at our solstice party as well. While you have tried to escape Christmas, I'm completely embracing it...all the music, lights, gifts and gatherings. Something that apparently only girls like, but nonetheless, I'm still enjoying it.

I'm trying to slow down my time in Vancouver, it's going v. quickly. I hope time is going slowly in the sun.

Xx lil booboo

Date: 10:44am Friday, December 24, 2004
From: Chad
To: Megan
Subject: Re: I tipped over the manger

Merry Christmas Eve,

It doesn't feel like Christmas here, but I'm glad you're embracing it as it is a lovely time of the year. We are going to Christmas dinner at a local restaurant owned by Canadians with other Canadians to have a Canadian Christmas dinner. How Canadian!!! Anyway, my trip is almost over, but the next couple of days will be great.

Christmas morning we are going on an ATV tour through some Mayan ruins and caves, and will do a little snorkeling. Anyway, Merry Christmas, and I'll call you Sunday night and see if I get ahold of you, as I know you are in party mode now. Matty's dad will be picking us up to save you or anybody else the hassle. See you in a couple of days. Chad

Mewwy Christmas

Date: 1:00pm Friday, December 24, 2004
From: Megan
To: Chad
Subject: Mewwy Chwistmas

Merry Christmas lil Chaddy!!

I'm glad that you are celebrating a little bit of Christmas...and with other Canadians. And snorkeling Christmas day –v. Christmas day rebellious! Will you and lil Matty "bite my lower lip" Stiles be giving each other little gifts under your tinsel-decorated palm tree?

Anyways, enjoy your Christmas, Chaddy...Merry Christmas to your wingman as well.

See you soon.

Long Hugs and Nice Kisses for you under some kind of Mexican mistletoe!

Meggie xo

I THINK YOU WERE PUT HERE
TO MAKE ME BETTER.

Once Chad was back on Canadian soil, the hugs and kisses I received were big and often. We followed each other everywhere we could, holding hands, linking arms—any way of leashing ourselves to the other, yapping like puppies.

Chad spoke only with optimism any time university came up. "You are going to have so much fun." "Your tennis game is going to skyrocket." "It's a great opportunity to buckle down, do well in school, and get it done."

I absorbed everything he said as though every sentence was gospel—knowing that if I paid attention and worked as hard as he believed I could, I would make him proud. I would be the girl he believed in, not the typical college girl he was scared I'd become.

He talked and held me as though—just for our remaining days together—he had let himself fall for me. I could tell he would miss me. The months of arguing had been a byproduct of him knowing it.

Then the time to say goodbye arrived. A few blocks away from my parents' house, where he was about to drop me off, Chad pulled into a shopping center parking lot. Reaching behind the passenger seat, he pulled out a small, brightly colored bag.

A gift! Really!?

Inside was a card - thoughtfully written, in a way he would never speak.

Well, my love, here we are again! I'm looking forward to what the future brings us. As long as it brings you happiness, then all is well on my end.

I wish you all the love and fulfillment I have to give. You are starting a new chapter, and this gift should help keep your new adventures clear in your mind.

I love you.
Chad

Opening the bag wider, I lifted out a box. My first digital camera!

"I didn't know what to get you, but thought you could use this to capture all the new memories you're going to make," he explained.

I was as thrilled by the handwritten "I love you" as I was by his thoughtfulness. Unable to smile any wider, I leaned over his Jeep's center console and threw my arms around his neck. "Thank you so much, Chaddy," I said quietly before pulling back. "I got you a card. It's nothing, just a card. Don't read it until I'm gone though, okay?" There was a calling card inside, and I hoped he would use the following day.

"Ah, you little turd—you didn't need to write me a goodbye card! But make sure you take good care of that camera. Don't be dropping it drunk or anything. And send me a few pictures."

Even though we both knew it was coming, the goodbye still felt awkward and unsure until Chad broke our silence and filled me to the brim with warmth. "You know, I think that you were put on this planet for me. I think you were put here to make me better."

All the difficult times had been worth it, just to hear that.

He pulled me in tight for a hug—just as big and warm as when I stood in his hallway on our first date. "Okay, Meggles, have a good flight. Call me when you land and be a good girl. Work hard."

"I'll miss you," I croaked.

"Me too." He let go, but kissed me once more before he walked back to the driver's side.

I followed. As the door closed, he rolled down his window. I held his face in my hands and kissed him one last time.

My Chaddy,

I'm not sure even if I know how to start this kind of note. Knowing very well it's not a note of goodbye, but more a note saying 'see you in three months.' I'm not sure how clear everything I want to say to you would be if I began to do my usual blabbing, so for efficiency purposes, I will make you a list.

A list of 31 things I want you to know, understand, and remember when I'm not around to say them.

1) You have done more for me these past six months than I thought anyone could do for me.

2) I love it when you smile. It makes me smile, too.

3) Even though I make fun of your apartment, I still like it, and have enjoyed every minute wasted there.

4) You smell gorgeous. Cologne or none. I like it.

5) As accidentally as "we" happened, you accidentally became my best friend as well. (I love that!)

6) Even though you were just trying to sleep with me, I adored our first kiss on that rock thing by the water.

7) I know you are happy for me, but if you miss me, will you please just call and tell me?

8) I believe (almost) everything you tell me on the tennis court.

9) Even though you think all women are crazy, and I've tried not to act like one around you because of that, but I am one, and I love it when you make me feel like one.

10) I will never be anyone else's pooky bear/booboo bear. I hope you will never have another one, as well.

11) I really enjoyed dancing with you for 4.5 minutes on New Year's Eve. You're a fun dancer.

12) I feel safe with you. Safer than I have ever felt with anyone.

13) I would never go to Harrison with anyone but you. I would never go to Harrison again.

14) I don't like it when you fart. But I won't let it bother me anymore when you do.

15) I'm going to try and not cry when I say goodbye to you. We'll see how that goes.

16) When you don't have your stupid "wall" up for self-preservation and you tell me how you really feel...I feel all girlie inside. I like that.

17) You got me to smoke. Bad boy.

18) I care for you more than I have words for. I don't know when or how it happened. I didn't know it was possible to care for someone this much. I wish you could know how much I wish you wellbeing, health and happiness.

19) That piece of paper sitting on top of your bed is a show of your hard work through college. I look forward to seeing the success you have using it.

20) As hard and stubborn as I act around you, you really make me a big ol' mush-ball.

21) I know I'm still a baby and have a lot to learn and experience, but this doesn't mean that I wouldn't like you around to enjoy it with me.

22) I know there are 9.5 years between us, but Celine Dion married a guy 17 years older than she is. So. There will always be others more pervy.

23) You make me really happy. Even during not-so-great times, I come out the other end (that is, one week later) happy.

24) I am a better person because of you.

25) I trust you with everything I have. I know you think girls are hard to trust, but maybe you could trust me, too.

26) No matter what wanting or waiting I did these past six months, you are well worth it.

27) I told you that I could see myself falling in love with you. Five months later, it's still true.

28) Whatever happens with work, success and life, you know I'm proud of you. I'm proud to know you. I love what you have done for me and I love that I know you.

29) I'm a big girl and know what I'm feeling. So thank you for being excited for me and reminding me of all the new adventures I'll have. But let me miss you. I want to. I do. And I will.

30) Sorry this note is so long, but you needed a little reminder (that you can whip out whenever you might miss me) of all my ridiculous thoughts for you.

I wish I could explain it all more, but somehow I think you already know.

Always, xx Your Meggie.

xx

Date: 2:24pm Tuesday, January 4, 2005
From: Chad
To: Megan
Subject: RE: leaving

Meggie,

I'm not sure what's happening to me. I tried so hard to prevent these feelings from coming out. I'm hoping you know something about us that I don't. I can't believe it took you leaving for me to feel this way. I had a tough day yesterday when I left you. I felt sick to my stomach. I hope you know what you are doing, because I told you it's going to be tough. Anyway, I hope you are getting sorted out down there in your new home away from home. Catch some rays for me. I'll talk to you soon.

Love, Chad

Date: 9:08am Wednesday, January 12, 2005
From: Chad
To: Megan
Subject: RE: DID YOUR MOM PACK YOUR LUNCH FOR YOUR FIRST DAY OF SCHOOL?

What, no email this morning...how disappointing. Hope your day is full of sunshine as mine is as cold as the far corner in Hell. Perhaps that was a bit dramatic!!! Anyhow, I do appreciate your clever little emails, so don't fucking forget. Again, a little dramatic, but necessary. Bye for now. Chad

TALK TO YOU SOON.

Chad and I missed each other so much, emailing and calling nearly everyday—for two weeks.

As we closed in on our second week of being apart, what we used to argue about inevitably happened. I became immersed in college life while Chad continued his grown-up life at home.

Chad became notably distant in our conversations, limiting his questions only to school and upcoming matches. He stopped asking about how I was doing and stopped saying he missed me.

"Do you miss me?" I asked one night.

"Yes, Meggie. Of course I miss you." He answered like he had been waiting for this opportunity. "But you're living your new life now and I'm still here. It's hard missing someone."

My stomach told me where the conversation was going, but it didn't feel any better when he said, "I think it will be better if we don't talk so often. But we'll still be friends and you can call me whenever you need it."

A sarcastic, "Great. Thanks." was all I could shoot out from behind my tears, even though I knew he was right.

I was surprised at how easy it was for the physical distance between us to support the emotional separation, but there were days, like on his 30th birthday, when I ached to be back in Vancouver where I could be his. Instead, there were friendly, flirtatious, safe-at-a-distance progress report emails once in awhile that I looked forward to. And the occasional bombshell.

Date: 7:57 PM Monday, February 14, 2005
From: Megan
To: Chad
Subject:

Happy Valentine's Day, chaddy
Xo

Date: 9:08 AM Wednesday, February 16, 2005
From: Chad
To: Megan
Subject: re:

Hello Meggie,

I'm starting to wish you never entered my life, as you are making it far more complicated than I need it to be. I find myself comparing people to you, which is a compliment to you, unlike the first sentence of this email.
Take care, Chad

Date: 8:04 AM Friday, February 18, 2005
From: Megan
To: Chad
Subject: you danced – all night?

Chaddinuga,

Please don't wish that I had never entered your life. We wouldn't have had very much fun if I hadn't. On the flip side, however, I needed to hear that you are having difficulty with comparisons as well. I am also suffering from the same frustrations and standards set by your little pee head and big balls. I would rather not try to count the times when I have said something amusing and realized you weren't there to reply with "ah, Meggie, you are a very clever little booboo bear" (and squeeze my head the way I loathe).

I'll talk to you really soon, Chad. Meggie.

PS. Call when you want a homie to chat to when you're chillin' on your couch watching Conan.

Date: 11:59 AM Friday, February 18, 2005
From: Chad
To: Megan
Subject: re: you danced – all night?

Meggie,

You know how I have felt this situation to be from the beginning – hopeless. The problem is I find myself comparing you to everyone I've ever dated or had a relationship with. Anyway, life is tough and things aren't always going to work out the way one hopes.

Enjoy Miami and get some sun for me. I could really use it. Well, I have to get on court. Chad

Date: 1:47 PM Sunday, February 27, 2005
From: Megan
To: Chad
Subject: ......

Chadabelle,

It was really nice to talk to you the other day.

I have to admit that I always thought that, when the two of us weren't together, it would always be the hardest on me. I never thought these feelings would be mutual. I'm so sorry. Do whatever you need to do to make things easier on you, and I will do the best that I can to maintain a "close, but not too close" friendship.

Just let me get this all off my chest: I still think about you every day and wonder what you are doing, and how you are feeling, and if you're happy. There is a girl who puts lotion on in my class, and it smells like you when you come out of the shower. I still have your advice floating around my head when I'm on the tennis court and wonder if you would be proud. I look at your picture every day and look forward to seeing you in a few months.

I'm not sure what else to say right now, so I think I'll just leave it at all this.

We can't take it all back, nor would I.

Xo

Date: 6:47 PM Sunday, February 27, 2005
From: Chad
To: Megan
Subject: re: you danced – all night?

Meggie,

Thank you for your concerns, but I'm fine. Life is tough and some days are better than others, as we all know. It was nice to talk to you the other day.

Also, it makes me very happy that you are having such a good experience down there and spreading that Megan Williams cheer.

I am proud of you because you are a very real person. Unfortunately, that is a rare trait in people of your age or even mine sometimes. I'm not sure how this all got so weird, but relationships are complicated. Anyway, keep fighting out there on the tennis court and don't give up. Play like you have never played before and take your game to a new level. Think about where you are placing your shots and when all else fails, attack the backhand. Anyway, you have a good week and I'll talk to you soon. Chad

Date: 9:25 PM Monday, March 7, 2005
From: Chad
To: Megan
Subject: just being a dickhead!!!

I said a few things that were just in bad taste on the phone tonight. I guess that was my way of making it clear that I'm not going to be here for you in the same way that I was before you left for school. I think you know that, so I'm not sure why I felt I needed to clarify that point. Anyway, I'm going to work on being a better friend to you 'cause you deserve that. I hope the best for you despite my rude comments and low blows, is what it all comes down to!!! Take care, little gal. Chad

Date: 8:58 AM Tuesday, March 8, 2005
From: Megan
To: Chad
Subject: lower your mutha fuckin' voice

You are a very strange medium-small-sized man and have an odd way of handling things that are out of your control. I can't decide if you are a weird friend or just a weird friend to me. Either way, I suppose that's not important, because it's just the way things are. I enjoy your weirdness and your weird friendship, so don't try so hard to ruin it.

Nonetheless, I still get a kick out of talking to you, so whether you like it or not, I will continue.

Meggie poo.

Date: 10:23 PM Tuesday, March 8, 2005
From: Chad
To: Megan
Subject: re: lower your mutha fuckin' voice

I'm bored running this league, so I figure I'll continue this absentminded conversation. I just reread your email and it got me angry again, so let's battle. I am not a dink, but I do want peace in my life, and you are not bringing me peace. I am not a strange medium-small-sized man, quite the opposite, hence the 15-inch cock. I do not underestimate you, as you are looking to have a piece of cake and eat it also. No chance my friend, no chance!!! Now that I have lowered myself to be a 20-year-old girl, out of boredom I might add: it is time for me to return to my infinite wisdom and end this message. You are funny at times, so I'll give you that, but the charms end there, sweetie. Peace out and good night. Chad

Date: 7:58 AM Wednesday, March 9, 2005
From: Megan
To: Chad
Subject: cool tools

You little penis wrinkle. You say you want peace in your life – don't think of only yourself. I want peace too, and you don't give it to me. SO. Stop complaining and just suck this up and don't expect to find peace anytime soon, because as long as I am not at peace with you, I'll drag you through the mud with me. You can try and hide from me, but you will never outrun me. For I am much more smart, witty, and cool than you. Don't bother wasting your time fighting it. The best way to take a hit is to move with it.

I am not surrounded by men, nor do I want to be, so stop assuming that's the case. As far as having my cake and eating it too – again with your self-flattery. What makes you think you are a piece of cake to be with? You are a mere cupcake, with a few sprinkles...and certainly no icing.

Peace in the Middle East,

meggiepoo

Date: 12:16 PM Wednesday, March 9, 2005
From: Chad
To: Megan
Subject: re: cool tools

Megan,

How am I supposed to move on with my life when I have you lingering around? You are young and have so much ahead, and relationships are a dime a dozen when you are 20. I'm 30 and I cherish all of my relationships. I would someday like to have a normal relationship that could progress into Something. So yes, I'm there for you as your friend, but that's it!!! Is that what you are looking for also? What are your expectations of me?

Really, though – what more can possibly be said about this situation? Hope the sun is shining down there, because it's raining up here. Chad

DID YOU WANT TO COME UP?

When I arrived back in Vancouver, it took less than a week for Chad and I to sit across from one another at the same restaurant we'd gone to on our second date.

"Look at you, all dressed in American," he remarked when I arrived at his place.

In my yellow polo shirt, matching flip flops and black skirt, his eyes made it known that he thought I looked as good as I felt.

Our conversation stayed cordial and polite, as if our agenda was "just catching up."

Until dinner was over.

Following last year's first date pattern, Chad drove us back to his place, where I had left my car.

"Did you want to come up?"

"Sure—but I won't be able to stay long." I actually meant it. My feelings for Chad had never gone away, but I wasn't interested in discussing any flings we'd had when we were apart. I worried that the more time we spent together, the more likely it was that our respective indiscretions would be shared.

We stood in his unchanged bachelor-pad hallway and looked at one another.

"There are those big brown eyes."

"You missed me, didn't you?"

"Of course, I missed you, Meggles."

I relaxed into his arms as we hugged.

"I missed that fine assssss." His hands smoothed my skirt, tightening for a squeeze.

Flattered, I swatted his hand away, "Is that all?"

"Of course that's not all," he said as he leaned in for a kiss.

I turned so he'd land it on my cheek. "What else did you miss?"

"I missed talking to you…and I missed kissing those lips." He smoothly aimed again and caught me before I was ready, this time landing his lips on mine, where they would stay for the next 20 minutes.

Every make-out has its tipping point, and when that moment came, 20 minutes after laying on top of him with his palms resting on my skirt, I lifted myself off and called it a night.

It was the start of another complicated summer together.

CHILDREN'S HOSPITAL

Dad was the first to be tested, and got through many of the preliminary stages before being told he wasn't a match to donate a kidney to my brother Bryn. Then my mom volunteered.

Perhaps if I had been a possible candidate (I was too young, among other reasons for being disqualified), I may have been more involved and supportive. But I wasn't. Bryn didn't look or behave any differently than I imagined most 18-year-olds did. He walked around—everywhere—with his shirt off, revealing his bodybuilding mass and the dialysis cord in his chest. According to his friends, the cord was a "bad-ass" complement to his many childhood scars. But most days, while I headed to the tennis court or the beach, Bryn would head to the hospital for the dialysis that was keeping him alive until a kidney donor could be found.

After months of tests, waiting, results, waiting, dialysis, waiting, tests, results, waiting, it was determined that Mom's kidney was an excellent match for Bryn.

Though the process of giving or receiving an organ is as serious as needing one, around our household there was relief, and hope that Bryn's health and quality of life would resume.

The date was set. Mom would donate her kidney to Bryn, whose body was now desperate for it.

I flew home from Jacksonville on September 20th, just three weeks into my senior year.

On September 26th, my baby brother (though 'baby' implies he's smaller than me - and that is about 60 pounds and six inches inaccurate) was admitted to Children's Hospital.

On September 27th, my mom was admitted to Vancouver General Hospital. She was prepped for surgery, because the following day she'd heroically donate one of her kidneys to her son, who was spending his days a few blocks away at Children's Hospital.

The morning of the transplant, Dad and I split up: I went to Mom, who would be coming out of surgery; Dad went to Bryn at Children's Hospital, where he would be prepped for transplant.

Mom's room was bright. The soft light of the fall morning lit up the pale blue walls, and it didn't look so bad.

Dressed in her robe, Mom slept, exhaling deep, painless breaths.

Perhaps because I'd watched too many episodes of Grey's Anatomy, I scanned her robe for blood, searching for some indication that she had just had an organ taken out of her body. But other than a small IV needle taped to her hand, her blonde hair and rosy cheeks looked exactly the same as she did before she changed my brother's life earlier that morning.

After making sure she was in good company with friends who had stopped by, I drove to Children's Hospital, where Bryn had just come out of surgery.

"I'm here," I said, calling Dad from outside the ICU's doors.

He came out of the automatic double doors. He looked tired and worried, but his posture indicated that everything was under control.

"He's in a lot of pain, so they are trying to adjust the amount of morphine he's getting." Dad went on to explain that everything went well, although they had a hard time getting through Bryn's abdomen because of all the muscle.

Dad pushed the big red porter's button to open the double doors as I assured him that Mom looked good and was resting comfortably.

I took my time walking into Bryn's room, reminding myself of his earlier advice: "It's super-shitty if someone arrives to your room crying. I feel helpless and I don't want to be the reason people are crying. Do it at home, do it in the car; just don't bring it here. It's too hard."

At the time, I had no idea how many hours I would spend in hospital rooms over the next few years, but I took his advice to heart and never forgot it.

The ICU was notably louder than Bryn's previous rooms; the electric buzzing from machines that kept babies breathing, the beeping heart rate monitors attached to infants, and the woosh of pain medications being automatically dispensed. I was not expecting this.

Then I saw Bryn.

I temporarily lost my ability to inhale. His body was larger than many men, but lying there in the portable bed, he looked so small.

His chest was covered in different colored pads with metal nipples, attached to beeping machines.

I felt like I was walking in slow motion towards him. When I got to his bedside, he felt me hold on to his hand and winced as he turned his head to look at me. He started to cry.

"Meg." He breathed out from under the oxygen mask. "It hurts so bad." I held his hand as if I was going to lift him out of the bed and carry him out of this noise.

97

I swallowed hard and blinked my tears back into my eyes, hoping he wouldn't notice. "You're doing so good, Bryny."

I did a quick scan of his body. Unlike my Mom, Bryn definitely looked like he had just had a life-changing surgery. The skin around his wrist IV entry was splattered with dried blood, indicating it wasn't easy to find a vein big enough to support the needle. The bandage around his abdomen was massive, and the tape and skin were smeared with blood-red disinfectant.

When I met his eyes again, I wiped the tears from his face and then used the same tissue to dab my nose, where the tears forced back into my eyes were flowing.

He was trying to get words out, but the pain only allowed him to wince. I searched his face, trying to anticipate what he was trying to ask.

I quietly rattled off answers to questions I thought he might have: "I just came from seeing Mom; she's doing really well. She looks great, and Sue is with her now. They're just chatting while she's resting." He blinked in recognition.

"And I've been talking to Concetta, and she will be here soon." Bryn's high school sweetheart had been a remarkable source of support for him that summer. Even though she was only 17, she was a source of strength for Bryn, something our entire family appreciated.

"Be ready to see her, she'll be on her way." He nodded before his eyes closed as a fresh burst of morphine kicked in.

I wiped the last of his tears from his cheeks, kissed him, and whispered with as much love as I could convey, "Keep resting and I'll see you soon."

The second I let go of his hand and turned my face out of his view, I stopped forcing my tears back into my head, and let it all go in the hallway. I felt an unfamiliar, bruised feeling in my chest: heartache. Seeing Bryn in so much pain hurt my heart.

I needed to call Chad. He was the first and only person I wanted to talk to. Resting against a wall, I dialed.

"He's all hooked up and crying, and they're saying the surgery went well, but he's in so much pain. I've never seen anything like it. The whole room is sad!" I rattled on. "And Dad said the area Bryn is in now is the same one he was in when he was a little baby."

Chad listened, and while he calmly acknowledged how big the surgery was, he also reminded me that though it's tough, it was also to be expected, "He had his fucking organs moved around, Meg. He's going to be in pain. But he'll get through it."

I had managed to completely ignore what would happen after the actual transplant. I never considered the pain Bryn and Mom would be in.

When I heard "recovery will take a few months," I thought it meant it would take Bryn's body that long to get adjusted to having a new kidney. I never factored in the pain that "having your fucking organs moved around" would cause.

I hung up the phone after agreeing to revisit the Thai place with Chad for dinner in a few hours. When I told my dad, he seemed pleased that someone was prepared to distract me from the day's intensities.

Though Chad and I were unclear about what roles we now played in each other's lives, the uncertainty was set aside as he simply listened and consoled me while I cried.

We were different than friends. I felt something toward him I couldn't express. And I believed he felt the same way. Like a couple that has been married for decades, we knew one another inside and out. We understood why the other behaved the way they did, why they said the things they did.

Yet it was all unspoken.

Dinner ended, and we walked to our cars without suggesting that our night go any further. There was a hug and a lips-only kiss before he reminded me to call him if I needed anything.

I got in my car and knew that I'd be calling him. I would always need to talk to Chad, even if it wasn't about anything.

Mom was out of the hospital in a few days. Bryn took a little longer, not surprisingly, but by the end of my week at home, his recovery was already well underway. I was able to get on the plane knowing that Dad had the support he needed to take care of them.

It's interesting how hospitals completely slow down time. When I returned to Jacksonville, I couldn't believe I had only been gone a week. Days in Vancouver had been long and unscheduled— a stark contrast to a schedule of morning workouts, two classes, lunch, two classes, practice, dinner, and homework.

But back at school, weeks of practices and projects became months of match-play and final exams, and I was soon packing a bag for Christmas holidays once again.

It always took a day or two before I'd see Chad, and we would resume our familiar routine. However, as accustomed as we were to this one-month-on, four-months-off dance, it took a little longer each time for us to learn the moves again.

Then, a week before I had to leave again, we'd find our rhythm and wonder why it had taken so long.

By the time I got back on the plane for my final semester, our difficult goodbyes had evolved to "see you in a few months." But we still exchanged handwritten, "until we meet again" cards each time.

The roller coaster continues, but we both seem to enjoy the ride (for the most part). I wish you the best and hope you enjoy every minute of your last year of college tennis. I will miss you but I'm excited for you. I think this will be a very energizing time for me also. Thank you for always listening and offering your opinion to me. It's nice to have someone to bounce things off of.

Well, here we go again. Take care of yourself and let's enjoy the ride wherever it takes us.

Love, Chad

I had been back and forth enough times to know that, even though our communication was sparse while I was away, he would be there when I came back.

At school, our tennis team was no longer simply made up of teammates—we were best friends. The eight of us made a supreme effort to squeeze every ounce of fun from our final semester together. And somewhere between matches and nights at the bar, I met two boys who held my attention for the remainder of the semester.

First there was Guy. He was a thoughtful, considerate, well-raised senior frat boy and we quickly realized we had two things in common: we were both about 5'5"—and we both loved me.

Then there was Rookie, a baseball player, who, for a short time, seemed as infatuated with me as he was with baseball. But after a night that included 21 missed calls, I decided Rookie's hyper-keenness wasn't high on my "things I like in a guy" list.

Guy and I spent the last two months of my semester in Jacksonville together. I was committed to him; I even let him call me his girlfriend. (I only called him my boyfriend among friends with an American zip code.) I liked him very much. I even said, "I love you, too" when he worked up the confidence to say it for the first time.

As much as I cared for him, and as much as he loved me, the forecast for our relationship's survival wasn't looking good once I graduated and moved back to Vancouver. He was from Jacksonville and would be returning to school in the fall to finish his major. I had no desire to stay in America and was ready to start a new chapter of my life.

We shared a tearful goodbye at the Jacksonville Airport, with a promise that he'd come visit Vancouver in a few weeks.

I was excited about seeing Bryn and my mom, who were both doing well. When I landed in Vancouver, it was hard to break my habit of calling Chad to let him know I was back, but I couldn't, because I couldn't bring myself to tell him about Guy. Ever since our first parting of ways, I had decided I would only tell Chad about a boyfriend if I was serious enough about the boy to let my relationship with Chad go.

Guy had applied for his passport and booked a ticket to Vancouver in the hope of delaying the inevitable end of our college romance.

So, I simply ignored the urge to contact Chad. I didn't call. I didn't email. I didn't text.

Then he got in touch. "Hey, you little varmint. Are you home?"

He did miss me! Dammit!

I waited as long as I could before I texted back. Three minutes.

"Yes, you dink. I'm home. Miss me?"

"Maybe."

That was exactly what I did and did not want to hear.

I kept my texts friendly and superficial, never surrendering to the urge to pick up the phone and talk to the friend I had missed so much.

When he texted, "Don't be a stranger," I decided it was an appropriate way to end to our disciplined, restrained conversation.

Guy would be arriving in a week, and I was determined not to see or have any meaningful conversations with Chad until Guy had returned to Jacksonville and I had time to think.

That plan didn't work.

The Stanley Park Open was the Vancouver tennis community's milestone event. There was a slim chance I'd run into Chad, but whether playing or watching, it was the best place to socialize with players home from college as well as my former coaches.

I went with the intention of watching my friends play, convincing myself that the reason I straightened my hair and wore my new green and white striped summer dress was because I was going to a ladies' league wrap-up party afterwards. *Not* because I might run in to Chad.

But I did see Chad. It did not take long for us to spot one another.

He walked towards me with a swagger that only Chad could pull off without looking like he was trying out for a Snoop Dogg video.

Relaxed, calm and cool, his saunter was complimented by his standard summer ensemble: sport shorts, t-shirt, flip-flops and his signature buzzed haircut.

"You look really pretty, Meggie," were the first words out of his mouth.

Stop holding your breath! Exhale!

Like a five-year-old who had been told by a Disney princess that she was the most beautiful girl in all the kingdoms, my face—not just my cheeks—heated up with a flattered blush.

"Thanks, Chad." Hoping he wouldn't spot my embarrassment, I looked down at my sandals and nudged a stone like it was the most interesting thing I'd seen in all my life.

Then I brought my eyes up to meet his.

Ah, shit. I was doing so well, ignoring you. But now I see you, I see those brown eyes and I still fucking love you. Now what am I supposed to do?

"Have you eaten? I need to get some food. Want to walk with me?" he asked, as if it hadn't been six months since we'd seen each other.

No! I can't go. Boyfriend arrives in a week. I want to, but I can't. But I couldn't say no. I didn't have a reason, and he'd think it was weird. I'll just say yes, and dodge anything that had to do with relationships or upcoming plans for the summer. Noooo problem.

"Sure." My stomach flipped. Here we go.

We walked through the tennis court parking lots, through English Bay's beach neighborhood to the restaurant he'd decided on for lunch.

"I'll have the Bolognese with the pasta salad, please." He ordered exactly what I expected him to. His simple taste in food was one of the small characteristics I liked knowing about him.

I tried to keep the conversation focused on him, dodging questions and offering vague answers to anything that might lead to a follow-up question revealing there was somebody else.

"What's that?" He pointed to my right hand, which sported a new ring. "Oh, this? It's a graduation gift from my mom and dad."

"Oh, I was thinking it might be from someone else." I couldn't tell if he was hoping I would elaborate.

"No! Absolutely not. No guys are giving me rings, Chad." I was so happy to answer truthfully, even if it wasn't the whole truth.

He picked up my hand to look closer and offered his review. "Well, it's really pretty. It looks special."

I fucking love him. I can't believe it! How is this possible! Guy thinks I love him, and all I can think about is that I never stopped loving Chad! Talk about timing.

Once we got back to the tennis courts, we sat on the hill in the late afternoon's sunlight to watch the matches.

My phone buzzed with texts from Guy.

"Whatcha up to?"

"At tennis now. Phone is dying. Call you later."

"Well, aren't you popular," said Chad. I took the hint—I was being rude. I switched my phone to silent mode and tucked it away.

I managed to keep the conversation simple and tennis-oriented for the duration of the matches, and afterward Chad walked me to my car.

"Nice seeing you, Meggles. Don't ignore my texts," he said as he closed my door.

On my way home after the party that night, my love's name flashed across the call display.

"Chad"

"I can't stop thinking of you in that pretty green dress. Those brown legs."

I don't know where the butterflies started. (My heart then my stomach? My stomach then my heart?) But my insides fluttered.

"Oh, really?"

"Are you still on the North Shore?" Sounded like he had a plan in mind.

"I'm just pulling onto the highway," I defended, hoping that I had ruined his plans.

"Why don't you turn around and come back to my place? Just a visit. For old times' sake."

My speedometer indicated that I'd slowed the car down without realizing it. I wanted to pull off at the next exit, turn back the way I had come and walk into his apartment looking as pretty as he said I did.

I pretended it was just mistiming. "Ahh, had you called a little earlier, you might have caught me. But I'm too close to home now. Thanks for the offer."

We spent another 10 minutes on the phone, me defending my decision and Chad trying to convince me to change my mind, but I made it back to my parent's house without turning around. But my heart? It had already turned back.

GEEZZZE LOUISSSE

Six days went by and, rather than seeing Chad, all I could do was talk about him.

I hadn't told many people about Guy out of fear that somehow Chad would find out. Some friends that were aware of the situation suggested that I tell Guy not to come. Others suggested I stick with the plan. "You have been away from each other for a while, so let him visit and see how it goes." And that is what I decided to do.

I would act as though Chad hadn't totally invaded my heart once again.

Guy arrived and, despite my feelings for another man, I was still really pleased to see him. Though, as luck would have it, Chad chose this week to turn up his efforts to get my attention.

"Hey, man eater. What's up?"

"Not much. You?"

"Thinking movie. Want to go?"

Yes, I do. I'd love to.

"Can't. Have plans. Thanks, though."

I ignored the texts, but couldn't bring myself to delete them. Sneaking glances at Chad's messages was a guilty pleasure.

Clearly dissatisfied with my lack of communication, Chad called a few days later.

When I saw Chad flash on call display, I breathed a silent thanks that Guy wasn't in the room.

I will not pick it up. I will not answer his call.

Voicemail: "Helllooooo......where are you!? Call me back. It's Chad. Bye."

Pacing the kitchen quickly and quietly, I briefed my Mom. Her eyes perked up as much as mine did when my phone lit up again with a text message.

"Geezzze Louissse, Meg! Playing hard to get?"

I showed her the message and we both let out a suppressed giggle at his carefully spelled out, "Geezzze, Louissse."

Guy surfaced from the basement as I clicked my screen back to black.

"Chad wants to know why you're ignoring him." Guy looked down at my phone, which had just buzzed in my car's cup holder.

"Ah, whatever." I took the phone from Guy, trying to stifle my excitement and panic as I placed it back in the cup holder.

Long moments went by without Guy saying another word to me. Dammit, Chad!

We parked in front of the liquor store. I searched Guy's face for any indication of anger or hurt while he looked out the window.

Then I realized he was blinking back tears. Oh, you have got to be kidding me...Is he going to break up with me right now?

That would be bad. Right?

Bad, but fine, too. Totally fine.

"I don't know why he's writing," I said. "I don't have anything to say to him. There isn't any reason for us to talk, anyways. I love you. He's probably just wanting to ask about some tennis tournament stuff."

We strolled the aisles of the liquor store separately. Trying to regain Guy's affection, I asked him if he'd prefer a bottle of white or red—in other words, what beverage will make this visit fun again?

By the time we walked out with one bottle of each, Guy and I were back on track to enjoy the rest of his visit.

On his last night in Vancouver, we marveled at the restaurant's mountaintop view while I contemplated starting the "this isn't working" conversation. Swirling the pale Gewurztraminer in my glass, I looked up at him and said, "If you didn't have to go back to school next semester and had graduated with me, do you think anything would be different about your trip to Vancouver?"

"I'd probably ask you to marry me."

Ohmigod. I swirled my wine faster, wishing my deep glass were filled to capacity. We were on such different pages. In fact, our pages were so far apart we might have been characters in entirely different books.

But all I said was "Wow."

I'VE MET SOMEONE.

"Hey. What you doing later?"

I messaged Chad the moment I got into my car after waving goodbye to Guy outside the international departures gates.

By the time he responded, I was gliding on the elliptical at the gym. When in doubt, work it out.

"Oh, now you answer me. I be chillin'. What's up with you?"

"Can I come over?"

I didn't care what his answer was. If he was home now, later or tomorrow, I was going to barge my way into his apartment the second I had confirmation he'd be there.

"See you then, you weirdo."

I arrived at Chad's apartment shortly after two. He totally is into me. He's missed me. He's going to be so happy I've missed him too. I'll tell him about Guy and he'll know he has won my heart.

Deciding against knocking, I walked right in to his foyer. He looked up at me, and though I couldn't read his reaction, I interpreted it as pleased.

He was sitting on the cream-colored couch that framed his living room, one hand resting on the back cushions while the other held his flip phone to his ear. Tanned and "chillin'" as promised, he sat with one leg athletically crossed over the other, wearing his old college basketball shorts and a tank-top.

I bounced over to him, ran my hand over his buzzed hair, and gave him a quick peck on the cheek before making my way to the other couch and sinking into my favorite spot between the two cushions.

He looked over at me as he spoke into the phone, "Actually, strangely enough, she's just walked in the door."

I tilted my head to the side like a puppy that had just heard its name being called.

Who, me?

I tried to guess who was on the other line. Who could possibly be so important he would keep talking once I had made my presence known?

"I don't know. No, she's back from school." The conversation continued without Chad letting on who it was or what they were asking.

"Yeah, she looks good." His eyes made contact again. He knew exactly the confusion he was causing.

I impatiently waited a few minutes longer for him to snap the phone shut.

Finally.

"Well, hello, Meggles." My insides glowed.

"Hi, Chad. Who was on the phone?"

"It was Rufus. He says hello."

Hi back, Rufus. I hope you told your friend that I'm awesome and he should love me.

"Where have you been?" His voice was teasing, but I knew he wanted to know the answer.

"Oh, just around. Hanging out. Went up to Whistler for a few days." It felt like we were in a Wild West stand off as we waited for the small talk to be over with and to get to the bottom of why I was there.

"So..." Out with it! "So, I was seeing someone in Florida, and he was visiting me this last week."

He started laughing. "Oh my god! I can't believe I didn't think of that! Of course you were! I can't believe I didn't guess. Is he still here?"

I lowered my gaze to pick at loose thread on the couch. "No. I dropped him off at the airport this morning."

He leaned forward and coughed out a laugh. "You don't waste much time, do you?"

"Well, I realized—after seeing you at tennis—that I..." I slapped my hand down on the cushion in exhausted frustration. Spit it out. "I realized that I never fell out of love with you. I totally still love you."

He slouched back on the couch. "Wow. That's not what I thought you were going to say." He smiled, but I was still unable to tell what he was thinking.

"So you just think you can come home after being away for six months, walk in here and tell me you want to be together?"

I didn't think I had left much room for interpretation between, "I never fell out of love with you," and "I totally still love you."

"Yes."

With both his arms stretched across the back of the couch, he smiled. "Well, I've met someone."

Huh? So? I'm home now and I love you, didn't you hear me?

"Oh? Who is she?" I didn't feel threatened, just very curious about the girl he felt was worthy of telling me about.

"She's a girl from work. We've been hanging out for awhile."

"Go on," I encouraged. Exactly who had been keeping my throne warm for me?

"She's super cool. I've had a crush on her for years. We're just talking, seeing where it goes." Ouch. For years? We had now wandered into territory I had not accounted for.

I tried hard to make sure I sounded interested, not jealous, as I inquired further. How long? How old?

He answered with more confidence than I would have liked. It had been a few weeks, and she was 31, just like him.

Chad shook his head as though he was coming out of a daze. "Listen, you little shit. You can't just come waltzing back in here after being away from six months, dump all that information on me, and think I'm going to drop everything for you. It doesn't work that way!"

"Why not?"

"Because it doesn't! You can't have your cake and eat it too!"

We came to a truce by changing topics, catching up, just as we had each time I'd come home before —and when I left Chad's apartment a few hours later, I was confident that whoever his "someone else" was, she wouldn't be around for much longer.

Little did I know.

Lady was a force to be reckoned with.

MORE OF THE SAME SHIT.

Chad continued to date Lady. While dating Lady, he dated me. While dating me, he'd talk about her. While dating Lady, he told her about me.

I started seeing a high school crush, Brad. When I saw Brad, I'd tell him about Chad. When Brad was seeing me, he'd tell me about another girl he was seeing.

From time to time, I would also hear from Guy. And Rookie.

Rookie had grown up (a little) since I had graduated. He was moving on with his baseball career, writing me from training camps, sharing what was happening with him as he was recruited to play for a pro team in New York.

We talked about visiting, but as I grew more settled in Vancouver and he started playing in the major leagues, we stopped writing.

Brad and I lost momentum before we really started. We were both just too involved with other people to focus on each other.

Then there was Guy. He missed me, and most of our messages were about just that.

From an outsider's perspective, this love hexagon must have seemed very twisted and strange. But in the middle of the swirling vortex, there were two points of stability: Chad and I.

Summer weeks passed with an abundance of frustration and excitement. Some days I was excited about the time I'd spent with Chad, and felt confident he would bring this weird open-dating season to an end and choose me. Other days, I was frustrated about being a friend he confided in. The grey area relationship-friendship gave me freedom, but no matter how many times I saw Brad, how many messages I received from Rookie, or how many phone calls I had with Guy, my heart was monogamous. It belonged to Chad.

During this bizarre courtship, Chad had shared that his health had taken a few dips while I was at school. He didn't explain much, mostly summarizing the drugs and side effects as "more of the same shit."

Despite the little information he shared, I knew enough to understand his body was struggling more than usual. Then, one day, in the thick of the August heat, he was admitted to the hospital.

We had been seeing each other less and less, and I wanted to be his go-to-girl. I wanted to know how he was feeling, what his energy was like, how he was sleeping, and what the doctors were saying. But I felt forced to accept the distance between us.

Chad's Journal
August 2006

I lasted about a year and a half on that treatment before my doctor pulled me off, as the neuropathy was getting worse.

What's next? A trial drug that is supposedly much more powerful, without as many side effects.

I started off okay on the Revlimid, but by the second cycle my blood counts began dropping. It is a common side effect with this drug, but after lowering my dose to keep my counts from getting too low, it was doing nothing to fight my cancer.

Now I'm running out of options. For the first time in several years I feel that dark cloud coming over me. I spent this past summer playing the local doubles circuit, and since I was taking no meds for the first time in five years, I was feeling like this was the way to go.

I forgot about one major issue: nothing was fighting my cancer.

I suppose I knew I was getting worse, but I was in denial.

I kept up my workouts and tennis but something wasn't right. DENIAL!

Megan

"I think I'm in the beginning of a relationship. You and I need to behave." Chad had sent the text from his hospital room, warning me off coming to visit that afternoon. I called for clarification.

"Hi. So what's that all about? You're in a relationship now?" I said, with as much mockery as I could to hide my distaste for his message.

He had the tone of someone who had made up his mind, but he said, "Well, kind of, I'm not sure. I want to see where this one goes. I can't do that if you and I aren't behaving ourselves."

The worried tightness in my belly loosened as he explained. It couldn't be that serious.

"I was going to stop by the hospital on my way home. Does that still work for you?"

"Thanks, but I think I'll be okay."

I failed to read between the lines, and said, "No, no, Chad, I'm totally happy to come by. Can I bring you anything?"

"That's nice of you Meg, but really, I'll be okay."

"I'm really happy to just stop in quickly and bring up some lunch, perhaps?"

Finally, sounding tired, he explained that Lady was on her way. With lunch.

"Ohhh. Okay." The tightness in my gut returned. I didn't like what her visit to the hospital on a sunny, summer Sunday revealed. She must like him. A lot.

I hated the fact that the person caring for him in hospital was an athletic, blonde, blue-eyed and successful woman—of his age. I didn't know what was more upsetting: the facts I knew or the blanks I tried to fill in for myself.

In addition to the tornado of a love story I felt twisting around me, my brother's health was declining again. Our family had been spun back into the "test, wait, result, test" cycle once again as they tried to figure out why Bryn's kidney wasn't working, just a year after his transplant.

Weeks went by before it was confirmed that his body wasn't rejecting the kidney. Instead, it needed reconstructive surgery, a procedure more elaborate than the transplant itself. When we found out, I called Chad, as I had a year earlier when I relied on his friendship to get me through. He listened and responded with calmness and maturity that reassured me with every word. "Meg, he's such a strong guy. There's no doubt this is serious, but everyone in your family is strong. You will all get through it."

Our conversations weren't long anymore, but they always left me feeling like Chad was in my corner—no matter who else was in his.

And he was right. Bryn did get through it, recovering from the surgery with the same strength and resilience he showed on the football field when shaking off a tackle. He was back on his feet in no time.

WHAT ARE YOU DOING IN HERE?

"Had a bit of a blip. Back at VGH."

After receiving Chad's text, I decided to make my way to the hospital one afternoon. I didn't care that he wasn't responding to any of my texts, nor did I care if Lady was there. I didn't have a good feeling about him being back in the hospital so soon after his last stay, and I needed to see him.

Judging by his surprised face when I walked into his room, he had no idea how I had found him.

"Knock knock," I said, walking through the open door. "Can I come in?"

The noon-hour sunshine drenched his hospital room with light, and I saw his face brighten when he looked in my direction.

"Meggles!" he said, with the affection I was hoping for.

"Hi Chaddy," I said, smiling. "So what you doing in here?"

He gave me an overview of the roller coaster of events: down to "the docs thought I was a goner" and back up to "but my counts seem to be improving, so we'll see if I can get out of here in the next day or so."

Your text said a blip! Not "goner!" Good thing I came.

Even though I'd been around for the ups-and-downs of tests, results and "blips," this was the first time I was seeing Chad in the hospital. He looked fine to me. I'm sure he'd disagree with that statement, but as I was completely capable of admitting, I always saw him through rose-colored lenses.

"Have you had many visitors?" What I really mean is, has Lady been here?

"Actually, you just missed her; she brought over soup but had to go back to work." Rats.

But if she was still in the picture, why was he looking at me like that?

The green and yellow flecks in his brown eyes seemed to catch every reflection of sunlight in the room as he gazed at me. He stood up from the bed, untangled the cords that connected him to the bags hanging from the IV pole, and slowly walked over to me, wheeling the pole beside him.

The chemistry in the room shifted.

All of a sudden I became totally aware of my hair—too frizzy? My teeth —did I brush after lunch? My shirt—too tight around my belly? Screw it. Whatever was going through his mind and causing him to look at me like that, he was not concerned with how I looked.

As he towered over me, I noticed the lines around his eyes. They seemed deeper, and lengthened as he smiled at me. Though his skin was dark from hours of coaching in the sun, he was pale beneath his tan. For anyone who hadn't loved his face for many years, it would be easy to believe that Chad was healthy and strong. I could see otherwise. He wasn't well.

He pulled me in and wrapped his arms around my shoulders. With my arms around his midsection, I pulled him closer. No matter how sick he was, he still felt strong to me. He dropped his lips down onto mine as he pulled out of the hug, wrapping one of his hands around my arm.

Whoooaaa! I soaked up the moment as long as I could.

Ending our kiss, he dropped his hand into a familiar ass-grab over my skirt, and bit his lip mockingly, Chad's usual way of signaling any level of desire.

I smacked his shoulder, careful not to disrupt any IV tubes.

"Chad! We are supposed to be behaving. That is not behaving." I was confused.

"Come on. How about a little 'tsch tsch' in the bathroom before the nurses come in?" I knew exactly what that meant. I also knew that, had I said yes to his offer, he would have been surprised.

But it was impossible to entirely rid my voice of flirtatiousness. "Chad! Not behaving! And I'm not going to give you a quickie in the bathroom with the nurses outside!"

"But I'm hooorrney!"

Brilliant. My opportunity had come: "Well, maybe that's something you should get your girlfriend to help you out with."

I tilted my head up, gave him a sultry kiss and whispered, "And we're being good, so that can't happen anyways."

I could almost feel a seal between us releasing as I stepped away and broke the tension.

Whatever it was, the connection between us had been re-established.

Chad's Journal
November 2006

I have women problems, real women problems. I've been involved with a girl over the past few months and she's been consuming my thoughts.

I've been through many emotions over her, and at this point things seem to be coming to a close. She maintains that she cannot get involved with me because of my health issues. I'm not convinced that is everything, but it's her decision. Who am I to say otherwise? At times I've been convinced I'm in love with her, but "I keep a close watch on this heart of mine!"

She doesn't really seem to have space for me in her life, yet she has spilled her feelings to me in letters and conversation. She wants to be my friend now, but I'm having a hard time accepting that transition. How do I go from intimacy—and maybe being more in love than ever just a few weeks ago—to friendship?

It's a strange situation because part of me now thinks that maybe I've just been foolish. Maybe she is not the girl for me at all. Maybe I should move on. I've tried lately, but she won't let me go. But I think now she is seeing it might be the only way. "Release Me!"

I'm fighting for my life, but I'm more concerned about her and how I wish she were in my life each day. I barely see her anymore. We speak each day, but I think that is coming to an end now, too. She leaves for Thailand in a few days and she'll be gone for three weeks.

There is someone else in my life, someone I can't explain. I've known her for a few years and she is really an unbelievable person. She is so much younger than me, 10 years to be exact, which has been an issue. That being said, she is always there for me and cares for me very much, as I do for her.

I enjoy her company, but my heart is somewhere else now. She even knows the situation with the other, but still hangs in there.

Life is crazy these days, but I'm still living. I might be facing my darkest days, but for the most part, I'm happy.

Depression creeps in here and there, maybe even daily, but that's only about death, so I'm prepared. Because at some point there will be nothing left to do for me. I'm fighting hard, though, and I enjoy the challenge. Bring it on. I'm confident that I might get healthy again.

I know that, physically, I'll never be the person I was before. But I'm becoming stronger and stronger mentally. I need to stay in this world for a while longer, because I have a mission. I know I'm here to help others and I'm trying. There is something bigger for me to do, but maybe I'm on my way.

Balancing everything in life isn't easy. Every life is full of triumphs and tribulations, but these are mine. It is time for me to stop pretending that everything is okay because everything is not okay. I've been hiding from my own reality for too long. It's okay to share your problems. Maybe others will find comfort. Don't get me wrong, I'm doing well. But I've spent much of my time fighting the issues!

MIGHT NOT BE HERE IN A YEAR.

For months the strangeness continued between us. We flipped between lovers and friends faster than you could say "love triangle."

"See, this is why you're so easy to hang out with. You're a little smart booboo, you know that?" he'd declare as I tried to help him figure out his relationship with her.

Now, I like to think that I'm a rather good judge of girl character. As Chad and Lady continued trying to figure out what was going on with their relationship, he confided the reason she was having such a hard time committing.

"She said, 'I don't know if I can be with someone who might not be here in a year.' That's so fucked up! I mean, she's taking away the only thing I've got by saying that. She's taking away my hope!"

I tried to see both sides. But no matter how I looked at it, I couldn't figure out why on earth anything like that would even come into her mind, let alone why she would let it come out of her mouth. The way I looked at it, if you knew what you were going to be doing in a year from now, you would have less room for love, excitement, spontaneity and good luck.

Chad not here? That was ridiculous.

I'M GOING TO STOP NOW.

When Lady left for Thailand, Chad and I had three weeks to play boyfriend-girlfriend. I was his date for a wedding, and we went to movies on Fridays and played tennis on Sundays. I enjoyed myself so freakin much.

I worked hard at keeping the time we spent together light and non-demanding, despite how badly I wanted to say, "So tell me all the reasons I'm better for you than anyone you have met and ever will meet in your entire life."

Three weeks without sharing her attention seemed like a long time at the beginning, but at the end it felt as if only a week had passed. I felt confident the three weeks Chad and I had together were enough for him to get over her, but I did have a smidgeon of worry about what would happen once she returned. There was no way he would just pick up where he left off with her...right?

Wrong.

Chad had never led me to believe that anything was different between us. We were simply enjoying our time together without the distractions of others. Meanwhile, I believed I'd have a land-slide victory and would be queen by Christmas. Instead, I had only been holding the throne warm while she was overseas.

We resumed the strange love triangle we had before she left.

But it only took a couple of weeks before I decided I had to pull myself out of the running.

It was a Friday night, and I had once again taken Chad's "maybe we can see a movie on Friday or something," as a definitive plan.

"Hello?" He said over a noisy background.

"Hi! Where are you?" I asked, hoping he was about to tell me that he was wrapping up something with friends and was ready to see a late show.

"We're at this underground concert thing." I could tell by his unapologetic tone that he didn't remember anything about his earlier suggestion to see a movie.

"Okay. I thought you said something about a movie tonight, but I guess you've already got plans," I said in a very 22-year-old, defeated way.

"Yeah, I guess so. Maybe we can try for Sunday night." I felt a quick surge of excitement before logic took over: another commitment-less non-invitation.

All in one breath, I replied, "Sure. Just call me later have a good time tonight," and clicked END on my phone before I could hear him say goodbye.

I sat in my parents' sunroom, Friday night, with no plans. Too embarrassed to call anyone and admit that Chad sold me out, again.

Then I had to admit to myself that it's not actually a sell-out unless someone has made plans with you.

I realized I was doing it all to myself.

I had been setting myself up with the highest possibility of getting wounded. I willingly put myself in the line of fire, and each time I'd get hit. I knew what was happening, yet it was me who allowed it to continue. Chad wasn't going to tell me, "Hey Meggie, why don't you stop cancelling your plans, because if you remember, I did this last weekend as well."

The wounds I believed Chad was causing were actually self-inflicted.

In a light bulb moment, I picked up the phone and clicked on his name from my recent calls list. "Hi."

"Hi." He sounded apprehensive, like he had guessed I was calling back to get angry.

The voice that came out surprised me. Sounding collected and detached, I said, "So. This feels like crap. I hate waiting around for you. I hate thinking that you're going to call, and then you don't. I hate thinking that you're going to see me, only to hear that you're too tired, or you've got other, better plans."

I continued before he could interrupt. "But I've realized that I'm allowing it to happen. I'm setting myself up for disappointment, so now I'm just going to stop. Whatever you and I are doing, I'm going to stop now."

"Ah, Meggie. Don't do that." He was sincere, but nothing in his voice sounded like he was about to put up a fight.

"I'm happy to still be friends. We can see each other when it works, but we will only be friends." I didn't want to be convinced otherwise. For the first time in months, I was making a relationship decision that would work in my best interest.

"Well, okay then," he replied. I snapped my phone shut with confidence and commitment.

MAYBE WE CAN GIVE THIS A REAL SHOT.

The night before he flew out for four days in Vegas with his friends, Chad and I sat across the restaurant table from each other with chemistry between us that had been missing for months, maybe more. We seemed to be buzzing with a mutual excitement to be in one another's company.

Maybe it was his excitement about his trip, or maybe it was my excitement about the upcoming Christmas season. Or mayyybeee, it was that our bodies craved each other. Whatever it was, it was electric.

Our dinner banter was drenched with familiar undertones of flirtation. And when there was a lull in chatter, our eyes kept the conversation going.

What I wouldn't do to stand up, walk over and kiss the head that holds that pea-sized brain of his.

Dinner ended 90 minutes later, and we drove back to his apartment, our palpable energy in tow.

Smiles turned in to a cheek kiss, which turned into a body-melting kiss. Before I could finish thinking "we were doing so well being just friends," the tension between us unraveled, fuelling one of the most romantic, heated nights we had ever had.

We laughed as we grabbed, gripped, pulled and held each other hungrily. My skin tingled in response to his kisses as his lips explored my shoulders and then moved lower. Later, as he lay on top of me, warming me with his long, muscular body, it felt as if we were the only two people in the world.

But once it was over, there was no sleepover, no snuggles. Just a lingering goodbye kiss, and I was out the door.

"Have a good time in Vegas. Give me a call when you're back if you want."

I woke up in my own bed to Chad's texts, updating me while he drove to the airport, waiting for the plane, sitting on the run-way, even while flying.

"Maybe we can give this a real shot."

He had been in Vegas for less than 48 hours and that was the message he sent. I read and reread that message. Over and over again.

Don't get excited. Don't be disappointed.

"I'd be open to that."

I couldn't help myself. I just had to go further.

"Though I'd have to see it to believe it."

"Alright then."

"Text me when you land."

I decided to surprise him at his apartment when he got home. The feelings of four nights ago were still on my body, and his note about giving us a shot was still in my heart.

"Just landed. Unbelievable. Worst travel day ever." At 2:30 a.m. I pulled into the guest parking outside his apartment. Adjusting the rear view mirror, I dabbed on lip gloss, doing my best not to look like I had just been dozing on my best friend Adrienne's couch.

I punched in his buzzer number and took a deep, excited breath.

Confused, he said, "Hallo?"

"It's me. Welcome home!"

"Meggie? What are you doing here?"

"Just wanted to say welcome home. Let me up!"

Had this been any other visit, I would not have knocked. We were both far more accustomed to me walking in without so much as a "come in," but tonight I knocked.

Chad opened the door, and I met his confused grin with an impulsive smile that made the lines around his eyes lengthen.

"Hi, Chaddy."

"Meggie, what are you doing here? I'm so happy you're here. I was hoping when it buzzed it would be you and not some drunken teenager trying to get buzzed up to his cousin's place."

He hoped for me.

I lay on his bed as he continued to unpack and vent about his terrible travel day. You'd swear that nobody on the face of the planet, in the history of flight, had ever endured such hardship.

When he had satisfied his need for compulsively organized unpacking, he showered and brushed his teeth, giving me a few moments of quiet while I lay comfortably on top of his bed.

I loved it in Chad's bed. His sheets were always soft and very clean, just like him.

He came out of the shower with a towel tucked high around his waist.

Grabbing underwear and basketball shorts from his meticulous closet organizer, he returned to the bathroom to change.

Though I'd seen his body a hundred times, I took his shyness as a sign of a fresh start.

When he climbed into bed, he pulled me in close and fell asleep, holding me as though he never wanted to let go again.

ARE YOU BREAKING UP WITH ME?

Chad and I had a wonderful tradition-starting Christmas together, and he surprised me with a beautiful necklace from Tiffany's. We rang in the New Year with his friends, as a couple. 2007 was off to a great start. Even with some discussion about me spending an indefinite amount of time in Europe following my cousin's upcoming wedding in June, Chad and I had never been closer.

In late February, I was invited to a family dinner with Chad's cousin Corey and his wife Raelynn, who were visiting from Alberta. Chad's parents joined us and we were tucked into a cozy booth at the back of the restaurant. I looked around the table at everyone talking and wondered if this was what it felt like to have in-laws.

Dinner ended with hugs all around, and arrangements were made for Chad and I to drive Corey and Raelynn to Abbotsford the next day. It was an hour-long drive and a nice opportunity to continue visiting.

But once we were in Chad's Jeep and out of earshot of his family, I could tell something was up. "You okay? You seem like something's bothering you."

Evidently very distracted, he offered an unconvincing, "It's all good. Everything's good." Not true.

"Have I done something to bother you? Are you breaking up with me?" I teased.

"I think so."

What the fuck? I looked and saw he wasn't joking. "What? No. You're joking." There's no way, this was totally uncalled for! We just had a nice dinner with his family. I met his cousins!

"Well, I don't know, man. You're leaving for Europe in a few months and don't know how long you're going to be gone for. And I think it's great you're going, but what am I supposed to do? Wait around for you to leave?"

Holy shit. I felt my face fill with heat. "Holy shit, you're serious. Seriously? You're breaking up with me? Now?" The disbelief caused me to repeat myself.

In that moment, I was angrier with him than I had ever been. "What? Were you just not going to say anything? Were you just going to let me guess that you were breaking up with me? What the fuck, Chad! Seriously?" I was caught so off guard.

He didn't have much to say. Similar to the way I kept repeating "what the fuck" and "seriously," he continued to firmly repeat, "I just don't see how it's going to work."

It was the same shit that I'd heard for the past two years: I'm too young, he didn't want to stand in the way, he didn't need this in his life right now, he's looking for someone who wants the same things as he does. Bullshit, bullshit, bullshit!

When we got to his apartment, I gathered my things quickly, being sure to get everything so I wouldn't have to come back.

I didn't want there to be any reason to come back: not for my toothbrush, not for a face cream, not for pajama pants. Finally, I uncoiled his building's swipe card and apartment key from my key ring.

It made me sad.

When Chad gave me a key to his apartment, it wasn't a fancy, milestone occasion. He just handed it over one evening. "Here you go. This way you won't have to wait for me to get off work if you want to come in to shower or hang out."

Putting the keys on my keychain wasn't a big deal, but taking them off was. He and I were no more.

I couldn't look him in the eyes. "Bye Chad. I'll see you sometime."

"Can we at least hug?"

I let him hug me one last time before walking to the elevator. I heard the apartment door close once I left, knowing he didn't watch me from his doorway as he normally did.

I was *so* sad. All those other relationships, the close calls—I never thought it would come down to this. I never thought we'd really be over.

I THINK I KNOW WHAT MY PROBLEM IS.

Bzzzzzzzz..... I looked at the phone beside my bed, expecting to see Adrienne's name on the call display. I assumed she was calling to check in on me after my tearful call to her last night.

CHAD

Was I dreaming? Did I forget something at his house?

I answered coldly. "Hello."

There was softness in his voice, "Hi. How are you? I don't know what happened last night. I feel really badly about it. I hated seeing you leave like that last night and I hated that you weren't around this morning."

I didn't respond. "We still have to drive Corey and Raelynn out to Abbotsford—can we come pick you up around 11?"

What the hell is going on now? Last night he was absolutely cold, and now he's asking if we can spend the afternoon in the car together?

A few hours later, he was opening the door for me. Driving along the highway, he spoke about 'us' as though we were still one. He looked at me with soft eyes that were both apologetic and affectionate.

As we pulled into the roundabout driveway at Abbotsford's Holiday Inn and said our goodbyes, I became more anxious about the long ride back. We were at least an hour away from home, and depending on what Chad had to say, it might end up feeling much longer.

We merged onto the highway and started the age-old discussion of why our age difference was such a problem for him. "Yeah, I know I am younger than you, Chad. Did you know you are older than me? And so what? Why is it such a problem for you? I put effort into you, so why was it so hard for you to put effort into me?"

Then, right in the middle of our calm battle, he interrupted himself. "I think I know what my problem is with you going away, and with us, and why I act the way I do."

Though I was used to hearing about many of Chad's problems with our relationship, my stomach tightened, bracing for another disappointing blow.

"My problem is that I love you. And with you going to Europe and with…"

Whoa, whoa, whoa, whoa. I beg your pardon!? You *love* me? I couldn't hear another word he was saying. I absorbed the three words I had hoped to hear for years while he quickly carried on as though he'd said it a dozens of times before. He loves me.

I was able to squeeze in, "You realize that's the first time you've ever said that to me, right?"

"What? Yeah, I guess it is," he observed before carrying on. "And I don't know, it's weird, it's fucking scary being this attached to someone. You have the potential to really hurt me and that's hard to accept."

I shifted in my seat so that I was close enough to lay my head on his shoulder. He knows I love him too. I hadn't done a very good job of disguising that, but his "I love you" changed whatever this was between us.

The last 30 minutes of our drive was wonderful. We drove past the exit to my parent's house and continued another 20 minutes down the highway to his place. Now that we had crossed this relationship threshold, time apart from one another seemed like the worst idea since breaking up.

That evening, I was getting out of Chad's shower, listening half-heartedly to his conversation on the phone. "Sure, I could probably meet up with you in a bit. I just have to drop my girlfriend off at her friend's place."

Girlfriend!? I skidded out from behind the bathroom wall to verify that it was actually Chad speaking. He didn't look up, therefore missing my goofy, toothy smile.

Girlfriend!! I wanted to jump into his arms and wrap myself around him in a front piggyback. I turned back towards the cabinet mirror smiling to myself. I was Chad's girlfriend. Chad was my boyfriend. Finally.

A TELL-ALL LOVE LETTER
FROM LADY

In the three months before I left for Europe, Chad and I finally allowed ourselves to fall deeply in love. It was exhilarating.

Anything from our past—other 'plus ones' that had existed—it had all been put to rest. One night in April, he demonstrated his commitment to burying the past.

Standing up from the couch, Chad walked over to his nightstand where his most personal journals, cards and notes were kept. He pulled out a folded letter.

Letter in hand, he walked to the kitchen, and returned with a plate and a lighter.

Without looking at the contents, I knew what it was. A tell-all love letter from Lady.

"This is the letter she told me she loved me in—I don't need that shit in here anymore." He held the letter over the plate and raised the flame on the lighter.

"Chad, you don't have to do this. You might want to keep it to look back on someday. Who knows? You won't be able to take it back once you do this. What if you wanted to read it again?"

I have no idea why I offered resistance to his gesture, but it didn't matter; he had made up his mind and he touched the flame to the corner of the pages. And up it went, from the bottom corner, to the center, to the top. I could see Lady's handwritten words transformed into ashes.

As though he had just tidied up crumbs from his dinner, he picked up the plate and returned it to the kitchen; and just like that, Lady and her memories were gone.

SEE HOW IT ALL GOES.

Mr. Booboo Bearskies,

I thought about writing you a long note telling you how I feel, how much I miss you and how much I love you...but I figure whatever you are feeling now is exactly how I feel.

I love you with all my heart and look forward to building a life together.

I'll love you forever. xoxo
"When I come back I'll wear your wedding ring."

The afternoon I got on the plane to London was tearful. We were both upset that the momentum we were building together was being interrupted by my long-anticipated Europe trip.

For the 90-minute highway ride from Heathrow to Loughburough, I had to close my eyes to stifle my jealousy as I listened to Concetta and Bryn chatter excitedly with my uncle. I was jealous that she was here and Chad wasn't, that Bryn got to introduce her to our family as his girlfriend.

As each family member arrived, I'd repeat a similar script, reciting the story of us: What Chad did for a living, how long we'd been together, and what he was up to while I was gone.

"You're going to have such a great time." Chad was encouraging when I called on my first evening in a different time zone. That conversation was filled with love and longing. But inevitably, like college, every conversation thereafter faded in enthusiasm. Once again, I was reminded that it was always easier on the person leaving than on the person staying.

Bonjourno Bello!

This is the Fontana di Trevi. It is right near our hotel. We were there last night when it was all lit up. It reminded me of an ancient Bellagio. Apparently if you throw a coin over your left shoulder you will return to Rome. If you throw another, you will fall in love. I did both in hope I can return to Rome with you.

If you throw a coin a third time...you are just wasting your money.

I love you! See you soon.

Bonjourno Chaddy!

Venice is beautiful and I can't wait for us to come here together. The city is really all divided by canals. I haven't seen a car since I got here. You will love it: cafés to sit outside, watching the boats, and funky Italian style...lots of walking, good food and gelato. I feel like I am in the movies. Where I (the princess) walk with you (the prince) down the streets listening to people singing, "When the moon hits your eye" then commenting on the stray dogs and over-friendly pigeons.

I love you with all my heart. I can't wait to be with you forever.

It had been weeks since we spoke on the phone, but I sent him a postcard, sometimes two, from every place I visited. Each one ended similarly: I love you. I wish you were here.

When I arrived in Hungary to visit my Jacksonville teammate, I realized it had been over a week since there had been any emails exchanged between Chad and I. Prior to that, his replies had been so brief that they reassured me only that he wasn't squashed under a tennis ball machine somewhere.

I picked up my friend's portable kitchen phone and dialed Chad's number.

"Well, hello there!" I chirped, hoping my time-zone calculations had been correct.

He was surprised to hear from me. "Hi!"

The chatter between us was quick, as he thanked me for the postcards and shared how he'd been keeping busy. Once I updated him on my travel itinerary, it seemed our well of topics had dried to its last drop.

"Well alright, princess, I should let you go."

"Okay, then… Bye."

"Byyye…"

Neither of us hung up.

"Why don't you say that you miss me anymore? Why don't you say I love you like you used to?" I blurted out.

"What? Jeeze, Meg, it's hard having you away. You're off there and I'm here. It's like you don't even consider that I'm left waiting for you."

It was as if all the support he'd offered during the months leading up to my trip had been covering a wound I had never noticed—a wound I was responsible for.

"I'm really trying to be supportive, but you didn't consider how I would feel about you leaving. You made all the decisions about going without even considering what that might do to us."

I wanted to dive through the phone, throw myself into his arms, and repeat, "I'm sorry, you're so, so right," until he believed me.

"I do love you, Meggie. And I really do miss you, but it's just hard to keep reinforcing it when you're gone. It really hurt when you left."

I needed to hear that. Hearing that I'd hurt him made me realize that I needed to accept the consequences of my decisions, and I tormented myself with thoughts of going home early. The opportunity to have an extended holiday in Europe wouldn't come along often, if ever again. I worried that I would be leaving my chance for the adventures of a lifetime behind me when I left.

"I miss you too. I'll call you really soon, okay?"

Two weeks later, I booked a flight back to Vancouver. Home was where my heart was.

"Ahh... Hi, Mr...Mr. Warren? It's Megan. Um. Chad's friend...girlfriend..." I wanted to bang my head against my steering wheel at how awkward I sounded.

"Oh, hi, Megan."

Oh, good. He remembers who I am.

"Um. So I came home a few days earlier from London to surprise Chad, and I know he's staying with you while his apartment is being renovated. I thought I'd call and see if he was at the house, or if you knew where he was?"

"Oh." Clark kept his usual steady tone, but his voice hinted that he was amused. Thankfully, he was prepared to participate in my scheme. "He left for the gym about 45 minutes ago, Megan. I believe it's the one..."

"Oh, I know the one. Thanks so much!" Click.

I pulled into the parking lot of Gold's Gym, and did a quick scan for Chad's green Jeep. Confirmed. He was there. I skipped around the corner of the weights section to see Chad, who had just finished his walking lunges. He looked fantastic: strong, broad-shouldered and healthy. With my new mauve, strapless cotton dress swishing around my legs, I walked towards him.

"Meggie! What are you doing here?" He was indisputably happy.

"Surprise?" I shrugged shyly, even though I wanted to tackle him like a linebacker. "I came home early!"

And then I got what I came for: the hug I had missed, but never forgotten. He mumbled something unnecessary, like how sweaty he was, but I didn't care. I was back. And as we walked out of the gym with his hand in mine, I knew we were back too—for good.

OFFICIALLY ROOMMATES

By the following Christmas, Chad and I were well integrated into each other's lives. Thanksgiving, birthdays, family events—we attended them as a unit.

Chad had stopped coaching tennis and had started developing a program for Hollyburn's high-performing junior tennis league, a desk job his body could handle. I was putting my college degree to use, working as the guest relations manager for a restaurant chain.

By the New Year, we decided it was time to leave Chad's bachelor pad behind and find a place together. He began hunting for apartments, picking his favorites for me to choose from.

"There are two places I've found that could work. I think I like one more than the other, but I want you to see it." He went on to describe his most promising finds.

"The one with the view," I said, without really knowing what I was talking about, having seen only one—the one with the panorama view of the ocean and city. So that was the one we chose to call home.

The first week of March 2008, we were officially roommates.

The learning curve was steep. Our habits clashed, and we certainly didn't share the same need to fold our t-shirts into perfect squares or sanitize the counter every time a meal was prepared. I loathed the way he corrected my method of Windexing the many mirrors he had installed on the new closet doors, and that he set aside all of Sunday morning for cleaning when it really should have only taken 45 minutes to clean our 580 square feet.

But no matter how many times I didn't do chores his way, and he apologized for being a "micromanaging asshole," I was lucky enough to fall asleep every night next to a man who told me each night - and about 10 other times that day - that he loved me.

Our housekeeping differences may have been a source of conflict, but they were easily outweighed by the small and yet significant things we agreed on. Like how great a noon-hour hit at the tennis courts near the beach felt or how cold Saturday mornings were a great time to bundle up and go out to get hot chocolate and a slice of pizza.

IT'S REALLY BAD.

We had started our lives together, and there was no longer any question about our commitment to each other, or how much we cared. We were together, we were in love, and it was forever.

As for Chad's health, it had been relatively good, and was certainly much better than the prior year. Leg cramps, low energy, and other permanent side effects from previous treatments were still evident. But otherwise, his cancer had been quiet, which was especially good news since he hadn't been on any kind of treatment for months.

After all the renovations to the apartment were completed at the end of April, Chad took me to Mexico, to an area of the Mayan Riviera that he'd discovered many Christmases before.

I don't know if he had intentionally timed the trip so that we would be away in the heat a few weeks before he had his annual bone marrow biopsy, but all we were focused on for the time being was the all-inclusive food, tequila drinks and the hot sun drenching our bodies. As Chad described it, "We be co-chillin'."

When we got back, I didn't go with him for his bone marrow biopsy. His description of the doctor standing over him, sleeves rolled up, driving a huge corkscrew into his hip was enough to make me think it was better that I hear about it afterwards. (Unless Chad wanted to be accompanied by the girlfriend who passed out while being "supportive.")

After the biopsies, Chad always came home and napped. It was the only evidence, other than the small bandage on his hip, that he'd been through such an ordeal. He had two identical marks on both sides—so small they could easily be missed—dark bluish-brown dots right on his back hipbones. The drill scars from previous tests made him look like he was mechanically engineered.

The thing with scans and tests was that we often held our breath for the results, and it took weeks before they came back and we could exhale again.

It had been a long time since his last test. And even though we hadn't talked about it, both of us knew the biopsy results were not going to provide optimistic news like, "Hey! Since you've been off treatment, your cancer is gone!"

So we held our breath until the results came a week later.

When I arrived home from work, I knew Chad had heard from his doctor. I headed straight for the couch, where he was sitting in his cargo pants and hoodie.

"So, how did it go?" Please be okay, please be okay.

He couldn't look at me. He was rubbing his index finger along the crease between his upper lip and nose as he always did when concentrating.

"I don't know what to tell you."

I could almost hear him trying to pull together the shaking on the inside so he could steadily deliver the news. "It's really bad. My counts are way higher than they were last year, and Dr. Nantal is really worried."

I knew what high counts meant: the cancer proteins in the bone marrow sample they took indicated how much cancer was in his body. I hadn't been expecting great news, but now my heart and stomach felt like they'd been liquefied. In an exaggeratedly calm voice I asked, "So what's the plan?"

"The doctors here don't know what to do. I don't qualify for the trial drug that my mom is on anymore, because when I went on it a few years ago my counts didn't change enough to qualify this time. They're saying there's a Mayo Clinic in Rochester, Minnesota, and they're going to get me in to see a specialist there. The doctors we have here are the best in Canada, but hopefully the specialists in Minnesota have a plan they can get me on."

As he rattled off the details, he seemed to be processing it all himself. "It's scary. This is the stage we never wanted to get to. I'm running out of options, and it's scary to think the doctors here don't know what to do with me."

He'd said scary more times that I wanted to hear it.

"Well, I think it's a good thing that, if they don't know what to do, they can refer you to someone who might." There was little positivity to find in the news he'd been given, but even if he was running out of options, there were still options.

"Yeah…" He had trailed off, far away, somewhere I couldn't reach him.

All I could do was slide as close as I could beside him, squeeze him into me as tightly as I could and wait until he came back to me.

He picked up his phone, sounding disheartened.

"Hey, Mom."

Fuck…his poor parents.

I heard half of their conversation as I watched his fingers repeatedly smooth over the strained wrinkles on his brow, "Yeah, it's not great. Is Dad there?"

"Hey, Dad." His voice was steady as he repeated the news, but had he been 10 years younger, I'm sure he would have been sobbing.

"Yeah, they're sending my all my files out there. They've made an appointment for me on Thursday."

Thursday? Four days! How serious is this!? I started wracking my brain, trying to figure out what I would tell my supervisor at work.

"No, no, I've got enough room on my Visa to cover it, but I don't know what the hell things are going to cost while I'm down there, so I'll let you know."

Jesus, I didn't even think about cost. Immersed in the Canadian medical system, we forget how lucky we are—never paying for a treatment or drug. I couldn't even guess what the price tag for a specialist visit at the Mayo Clinic would be.

"Thanks, Dad. I'll call you tomorrow."

Within minutes of hanging up, Chad was back on the phone, confirming the details of his appointment.

I busied myself in the kitchen, trying not to jump in and ask questions, but the fact that Chad was booked in as quickly as he was made me recognize his situation might be even more serious that I thought.

ANOTHER TRANSPLANT

Chad decided it would be best if I stayed at home and saved my vacation days for a summer trip together. I was okay with the decision, because despite the many warning signs, somewhere in the depth of my optimistic soul, I was confident a solution would be found.

It was a bit of a surreal week. I continued to work while Chad was finalizing his itinerary for Rochester. He would be gone for no more than four days. I would continue moving through my regular routine, like a robot.

I was very tight-lipped about Chad's ordeals, although I really don't know why. I guess that, until we knew more, I felt there wasn't much to say.

I even thought about not telling my parents, but only held out a few days until they asked something about Chad, and I had to tell them where he was. Since the start of our relationship, I'd always been shy about sharing information about his health with them. As loving, protective parents, I knew they hoped their daughter could lead a carefree life, something that was less certain with an older man, let alone an older man with cancer.

"It was impressive," he said, recounting the details once he was home again. "I had a really cool female doctor who understood my situation. She was positive and encouraging. She feels we can be really aggressive with this thing because of my age, and that we can get me ready for another transplant."

Another transplant. Another transplant! Transplants were good! Something that could offer a fresh start, rather than drug treatment after drug treatment.

"Apparently they've done a few second bone marrow transplants down there, and they think it might be my best shot at living a longer life."

His voice was lighter than it had been two days earlier. A plan, anything we could grab on to, was a positive. And this plan was it—a second transplant.

WHAT A GRIND!

Chad's Journal
June 2008

Well, shit. Here we are again! I wish I wrote in this journal more often. I suppose I spend most of my time just trying to live my life, ignoring the fact that this disease is wearing me out. I'm tired from being so unwell and from pure mental fatigue.

I just got back from a visit to the Mayo Clinic in Rochester. I met with a wonderful doctor who put together a few treatment options for me. My doctor here seems to have run out of ideas.

My heart is racing and I need to get on some treatment. I can feel I don't have much time, so tomorrow morning I start on some high-dose steroid treatment. They need to build me up so I can start chemo and thalidomide.

You know, I don't even want to discuss treatments, because it's fucking boring. I need to live my life, be a productive member of society. All I seem to be doing is getting by, although I have definitely been trying.

I really want to get my own business and investing off the ground. My dream is to be financially stable enough to focus my energy on raising money for less fortunate cancer patients.

I've been so lucky compared to so many people out there. I live in the city and have my parents close by for support. I've met so many people over the years that live up north or on the island. They have to pay for accommodation, transportation and even meds in some cases. They are away from family and loved ones while enduring their treatments. I feel for them, and I want nothing more than to start a fund for them. Wish me luck!

I need to write about my beautiful girlfriend Megan. What a girl, to put up with me. We have quite a story and I'm so lucky it has worked out. I believe that earlier I wrote about another girl, but that person only led me to Meg. Life is a comedy show, and you never know where the next act will come from. What a grind!

It's Day 3 of my new treatment from the Mayo Clinic. Wow, this is a doozer of a ride. I will never be able to put into words the trip I'm on. My emotions are everywhere; I'm just trying to keep it together. I'm succeeding, because nothing will ever beat me in this way. It is my mind, my happiness, my fulfillment, my love and my life!

As long as I'm breathing I will continue to strive for the things I'm meant to do in life.

In the end, life will go on whether I'm here or not, but I sure as hell will have an impact on it. Megan is strong and can handle any situation. I can focus on the task at hand: SURVIVAL, REMISSION.

What I wouldn't give for a few years remission. I would be so different this time around. I spent so much time in denial before that I didn't fully appreciate that period of my life. I'm embracing life like never before, and that is all I need to do.

I have to let these drugs take affect, so I'm embracing them also. I'm not fighting them, because they'll win. If I let them do to me what they are doing I win! Nausea, fatigue? I got the herbal remedy.

If I was a better writer, I would put something down in this journal that might be beneficial to someone, but for now I'll just keep mumbling.

Megan

The plan was terrible: one week of steroids, one week of chemotherapy, one week of Thalidomide. Repeat. Fucking terrible.

The second week of chemotherapy was a hard crash from the "up" of the steroids the week before. It left him nauseous, weak and without appetite.

By the time the third week of the cycle rolled round, Chad's body was the bloodied victim of the beating it had taken for the previous two weeks. Mealtimes were one of the only priorities. Though the steroids made him eat like an 18-year-old college student, the week of chemo and Thalidomide suppressed his appetite to a point he almost had to be force-fed.

Depending on how he felt each day, sometimes he'd eat his packed lunch at work before coming home to nap. Other days, he'd come home to eat just enough to qualify as a meal before dozing on the couch to recharge his energy. On good days, he'd peel himself from the couch and make it to the gym for whatever workout he had the strength to try.

As we entered the third rotation of his three-week plan, it became clear to me that his workouts were the biggest emotional upset for Chad.

Steroid weeks gave him the boost he needed to feel capable and "normal" at the gym. By the cycle's third week, I could predictably see the discouragement in his face. He'd build up in the first week and get knocked back again during weeks two and three.

He said it was like he was running on a treadmill, "Working, but getting nowhere."

As a couple, Chad and I did really well through the first two months of the plan's cycles. But the plan was relentless and unforgiving to Chad's body, and the ramifications began showing in our relationship.

He'd try to help me understand the mood swings that the steroids were causing. "They make me crazy. I don't know how else to explain it to you. It's like they take control of your mind. It's fucking crazy, man."

One Sunday afternoon, as we were about to go for a walk-hike, I put on flip-flops. He told me to wear runners. I told him I didn't want to.

It wasn't even like one thing lead to another; it just burst. He threw his lunch kit at my feet, "You know what? Fuck the whole thing. Don't even bother."

"Fuck you!" I cried. I punted the kit back at him.

He growled, "Jesus Christ, Meg. Fucking fine."

"Go by your fucking self, you asshole! You know I'm trying here! Why the fuck are you being so mean?!"

I cried when I was frustrated. It had always been my default reaction, and this debacle was no exception. I was so pissed off at him, but I hated yelling at him.

He felt terrible. His remorse filled every strained line on his face. We both apologized and went very solemnly on our walk.

Though it would not be the last time we fought like that, we tried. We tried our best not to let the treatment get the better of us.

YOU'RE GOING TO BE
JUST FINE.

As the first week of December arrived, the countdown to the transplant began. The cycles of treatments had worked as the doctor at the Mayo Clinic had hoped it would, keeping the cancer controlled enough to give his second bone marrow transplant the best shot of taking. After leaving work a month earlier, Chad had made getting strong enough for the transplant his only goal, and he had accomplished just that.

A few evenings before being admitted to hospital, we had some Chinese stir-fry dish he was craving from the mall's food court. (As much as food-court cuisine grossed me out, I decided that whatever the man who'd be turning away hospital food for the next few weeks wanted to eat, the man should get.)

Somewhere between, "How's the chicken" and "Ready to go?'" we acknowledged the upcoming transplant on a level we had never gone to before.

His eyes met mine while he stabbed his fork into over-sauced broccoli. "How are you doing with all of this?"

Throughout our relationship, Chad and I had talked a lot about our feelings for one another, but we had almost never talked about our feelings about his illness. So when he asked how was I doing, I guessed: "Fine?"

"But I dunno." I admitted, looking down at the squares I was folding my napkin into. "I just don't know what to expect. But how are you doing?"

Why I hadn't thought to ask this long ago, I don't know.

"It's scary stuff. It's a big risk." His tone was serious, "By doing this, I'm either lengthening the rest of my life, or shortening the end of it."

Life? End?

Tears. They filled my eyes instantly.

Chad reached across the short table and put his palm on top of mine.

"Meggie, this isn't going to be easy. If I get through the transplant, the recovery can be the most difficult part. The possibility it doesn't work is just a reality of my situation."

If you get through the transplant part? *If?* In a few days, Chad would be admitted into the hospital for an indefinite period of time—and only now am I starting to realize what was about to happen? There's a familiar word for this... Oh, yes—denial.

"But you're so, so strong, Meggie. I know you're going to be just fine."

At the time, I thought he was saying I'd be fine when he was in the hospital and recovering afterward.

I didn't realize until later that he was also referring to my life if he didn't make it through the transplant.

"Sometimes I wish I remembered more about what happened, and how long the recovery took.

"This time my recovery is going to be better. I'm going to do it right this time, and give my body the chance it needs to make this work for a long time."

Chad wasn't able to recall much more than a few vivid memories from his first transplant, and when the day came when he was to be admitted to hospital, we were both wishing we knew more about what to expect.

Chad had tried to keep a journal during his first transplant, but I knew how dissatisfied he was with the little he'd written. From what I understood, while trying to rest, barfing, trying to find strength to eat and re-learning how to develop muscle, writing a journal was the last thing he wanted to do.

In the likely event the same would happen this time around, I decided that I would help him by keeping a journal documenting the bumpy road ahead.

"One day you can read it. When you're better—when you're ready. And I'm going to take photos. Even if you don't want me to. I want you to remember how strong you are and how hard you've worked."

I watched him nod in his thinking position, resting his index finger over his top lip. His instinct was to reject the idea of photos altogether, but I could see he knew it was a good idea.

"Fine. We'll see, but it sounds like it will be fine."

I AM SO SCARED YOU
MIGHT DIE.

Megan's Journal
December 8, 2008

Dear Chad,

I'm writing this journal because I'm worried that in 10 months from now, or 10 years from now, I'm not (and we're not) going to remember the details of this past month. I will write this to you, because you're the person I want to tell everything to anyway.

I'm not sure when I'm going to show you, I just know that I'd like you to read it someday.

Perhaps when our wounds aren't so fresh....

I had a good cry a few days ago about everything I am scared of and everything I don't know.

How long will you be in the hospital? What happens, and how sick will you get after the transplant?

I know how risky this all is, and you and I haven't really talked about it...but I keep thinking. I keep crying about this stupid idea floating around my head. What if you die? I am so scared you might die.

When I drove you to the hospital today, I remember thinking that I'll probably be really sad on the way home. I wasn't. After our mall talk I felt ready to face what is coming our way; to get our game faces on. I wonder how you were feeling. You looked so brave and confident. You're so calm and cool. You make me so proud of you.

I felt so badly for you this entire week. Getting hooked up to all these drugs and machines, not being able to leave your room. And all the while having good energy, feeling "normal." I was so proud, watching you work out with those workout bands. I admired how determined you were.

Geez Louise!

WE HAVE A LONG
ROAD AHEAD.

Chad's Journal
December 9, 2008

Weight 73 kg
8 days from transplant

Christmas is 16 days away, and thanks to some last-minute shopping with Meg, I managed to get most everything done before being admitted. Now I need to find something good for Meg... Hmmm!

I'm watching the stocks closely and waiting to pull the trigger on the final 12% of my investments before Christmas. One more drop and I'm in!

Also waiting to hear from a contact in the hope of getting a donation, a step towards my goal. It's not going to be easy to get $1 million together, but I'm just thinking of reaching the goal. I'll get there, but I need to get out there and ask.

As for me and my condition, things are going okay. I received my first dose of chemo to begin lowering my immune system. I'm being pumped with plenty of fluids to keep my kidneys in check, and received two pints of blood and many other things to keep things me in balance.

Waiting for Meg to come back from a movie so we can have some time together. I think she is staying over, as she did last night. I enjoy that, but I don't want her to get burnt out, as we have a long road ahead.

Jesse Smith came to visit, followed by Adrienne and the return of Meg.....yay!

- Light exercise (need bands)
- Shower (need soap + towel)
- Laptop (need internet hookup)
- 169.4 lbs (77KG) on Day 2

Diet:
- Muesli for breakfast
- Baguette with smoked turkey s/w lunch
- Pasta/prawns for dinner

December 10, 2008

Weight 80 kg

Making muesli, and the big news is I can leave my room and venture around the ward. I'll be receiving two of my treatments today:

Fludaraline

Compath

Ewwwwey...that was a bit of a struggle but all is well. Lots of drugs, some shivers and napping. I had a nice surprise this afternoon as Cezanne walked through my door for a visit. So good to see her, as she and her family have been going through hell. Anyways, we had a nice chat and it was so nice to talk to her.

Big day for me as Uros is on his way up for a visit, so I'll be back later.

December 11, 2008

Tough night last night but finally asked for some Benadryl to cure the itches. (Chemo side effect).

I had some visitors this morning, including Stephen, Diana and Vanessa. I had a good chat with them all. Van and Di brought me a vibrating neck cushion, perfect for my travel plans.

Now I'm getting my treatments, crossing my fingers that I don't get any side effects. I also just completed a walk around the ward and some strength training using strength bands...good times.

My good friend JJ came by around 9:00 p.m. It's good to see him as he has been having a rough go the past few months. He's one of my favorite people and a great guy to chill with. I'm really looking forward to getting back on the courts with him.

My wifey returned to spend the night with me for the fourth night in a row, what a lady. I hope she is hanging in there; she is tough to read. She has so much energy. I want to be able to try to keep up as much as I can. She's amazing!

December 12, 2008

So much Benadryl to take care of the itchies but I managed to get a workout in between all the drowsiness.

My parents are on their way to see me, which should be nice as I haven't seen them in a few weeks.

They arrived with a sandwich and a gift for Meg and I. They looked well-rested and tanned from their trip to Hawaii. The rest of my day was pretty boring, so nothing else to report except I'm bloated!

Good workout and shower!

December 13, 2008

Weight 82.40 kg

Woke up early to a nice surprise: Meg showed up with some breakfast—very sweet of her. Later on Jesse and Adrienne brought me Quiznos and a Christmas ornament to hang cards and pics on. Jesse grabbed me some magazines also. Very cool of them.

I had another good workout and shower. Still very bloated, which is very uncomfortable, but it is for the benefit of my kidney they say. Otherwise just fighting the itchies from one of the chemos.

Excited for Meg to come later!

December 14, 2008

Woke up to some snow this morning, which was nice. I'd just like to get out for a walk in it. Meg and I had breakfast together and fell back asleep, a nice Sunday on a cold day. I can see Mt. Baker from my room and the rest of the Washington mountain range. I envision skiing down one of those mountains, but I will have to wait until next season.

My parents are on their way with a sandwich for me; looking forward to that. God the things that excite you when you're stuck in a room. I had plenty of visitors today, which was nice and kept the day flowing. My parents came by for a great visit followed by Uros and Sandra followed by Bryn and Jared!

I had time to get my workout and shower, which is crucial for my routine in here. I'm still in shock about how much fluid they have allowed me to retain. I'm carrying so much extra weight that I barely recognize myself.

December 15, 2008

Had my first dose of Malphalon this morning…good times.

I also had some surprise visitors around 1:00 p.m.: my old work crew Sharon, Tony, Audie and Tess, who brought me gifts and a healthy lunch. So good to see them all, as we always have a good laugh. They are definitely the part of Hollyburn I really miss. They were the reason I stayed as long as I did.

Good workout, followed by a quick visit from Dad, then into the shower. Went for a walk around the hospital and even stepped outside to get some fresh air for a moment.

December 16, 2008

I'm struggling today, with no energy whatsoever. The chemo has caught up with me but thank god that will be it. I start rejection therapy and will have my transplant the day after tomorrow.

I made my breakfast and lunch today and even went for a quick walk around the ward. I will just continue to rest for the remains of the day.

My weight is down eight or nine pounds after an entire day of Lasix. At least I don't feel as bloated—another 12 or 14 pounds to go.

December 17, 2008

Still 80 kilos, which is tiring me out—water balloon!

Lots of ice and a lil snow out there it seems. Meg and my parents are coming for lunch, which I'm looking forward to. Looking forward to having Meg around all day to hang out with. I need to figure out what I'm going to get her for Christmas.

I'm not receiving anymore chemo—the highlight of the day. I will have my stem cell transplant tomorrow night sometime. Things have been going fairly well so far but the hard part is still ahead. I'm focused on recovery and the thought of having some freedom from treatment excites me. To be able to accomplish my fundraising goals for 2009 and venture off for some travel after the Olympics is driving me. You know—so much is driving me that those two things are just icing on the cake.

I want to give Meg the life we dream about. I want to be successful in whatever I put my mind to. Hopefully we are on our way!

CHAPTER 43

TOO EMOTIONAL

Chad's Journal
December 18, 2008

Transplant was supposed to be at midnight, but flights were cancelled around the world because of the weather; the flight carrying my new bone marrow was delayed.

This makes me nervous but I remain focused on the task ahead. I had a good visit with Corey in the morning and my parents in the afternoon.

My Meggie returned to me in the evening, which always makes my day! Jesse and A also came by for a quick visit. It was nice. It was at this point I received the most generous gift of my life. Meg had worked hard to encourage 25 people to become bone marrow donors. I was so overwhelmed and still am as I look through each card.

I won't even try to put into words what this means to me and how special Megan is to me...too emotional.

I'm so lucky!

Since you've been sick, we've known not what to do,

So we've registered our bone marrow in thoughts of you.

Lots of love,

Your support team

I love you because you love my Megan, care for her and make her laugh and because you are her best friend. (Only when I am away!!) I can't wait to see you two again when I am back in Vancouver!

PS. I hope I have high-quality bone marrow!

xoxo Devora

Chad!

Insert Megan singing: "Don't stop believing—hold on to that feeling." That's the U.S. Open theme song from 2008!

Have a very merry Christmas!

Love, Carolyn and Rik

P.S You are fired from getting Letterman tickets this year.

xo Carolyn

Merry Christmas, Chad. I wish you a speedy recovery so you can get back to poker and we can share in your wealth!
- Jason, Cathy, John and Kristi

Hope it's a match!
- P

Chad, To your inner flamer.
- Love, Jesse and Adrienne

Dear Chad,

I hope this challenge proves successful, and that you are able to live the life you deserve. I really wish I could be there and see you. You are an inspiration and the strongest person I have ever known. I know there are many other people out there who will say the same thing.

Keep smiling that smile and if you are feeling down, just remember the time that I made you laugh so hard you fell off your chair!

Yours truly, Katharine

P.S. The Sedgwicks are with you, ALL of us.

I hope my bone marrow is as useful to you as my hand is on Megan's ass.

Love, Todd

Here is some of my bone marrow for you to enjoy.
Don't spend it all in one place. Xoxoxo, Diana
P.S. Merry Christmas. You're awesome.

I love you. You have changed my life forever. I
hope one day I can change someone else's life, too.
forever & always, Megan

One
Name
Even One
Might Change
Absolutely Everything
To a person in need
Chad, I hope that one day I can
Help somebody as wonderful as you
Love Karen!
xox

Chad!
This is the third card I'm signing for you this
season…You better F&*%in have a good rest and see
you soon! Uros

Chad,
We are thinking of you and pulling for you. We
love you, and just say the word if you need anything.
Love, Sandra

Hi Chad,

Dan and I both want you to know we are thinking of you a lot right now and have our fingers crossed for tomorrow. We are both really excited to let you know that we are going to donate bone marrow. I am able to, despite not being able to donate blood. We have signed up with OneMatch and sincerely hope that one day we can be a match for some other great person too. Continue to fight hard and well. All our thoughts and wishes are with you and Meg. xoxo Christy and Dan

THIS IS IT.

Megan's Journal
December 19, 2008
REAL TRANSPLANT DAY!

There was a little bit of nervous energy, enhanced by the phone calls and text messages of "good luck" and "thinking about you."

You sent me to go get soup, and on my way back in, the German doctor said, "You are missing all the action." I panicked a little, but when I came into the room and saw you on the chair talking with the nurse, my heart relaxed. What looked like a little bag of red blood hung from your IV pole, dripping slowly into your body. And that was the transplant. Talk about anti-climatic! After the transplant was done, and the nurse had left, you told me what the doctors had come in and said to you before the transplant.

You were a bit teary telling me how happy they were with your counts, how well your kidneys were functioning and how on track things were looking. Then you started crying.

My heart melted seeing how much you've been holding in. You've been so tough through all the bad news. You said you hadn't heard any good news in four years, and you've worked so hard for this.

As we cried together out of relief and happiness, you said you were getting cold. Then the shakes came. I lay on top of you on your bed, trying to warm you and suppress the shakes. Your teeth were chattering.

You later told me that, at the time, you were thinking, "This is it. The transplant has failed, and I didn't even make it through the day."

I can barely think about that now without getting a huge lump in my throat.

Later, you still felt shaky, but less and less so as you ate and walked around. Thank goodness.

All day you got texts and phone calls. I did, too—you sure had a lot of people sending their good vibes your way.

When you felt better, Alyssa came by and she and I went out to grab a bite to eat.

It's crazy to think that seven years ago, Alyssa was the one who told me you had been diagnosed with cancer.

You have been fighting for so long!

Chad's Journal
December 21, 2008

Struggling, feeling poopy!

Received blood and platelets and started morphine to release myself of general aches and some back pain. Still eating okay, although I wish I had more food around. Managed to keep my shower streak alive.

Corey and Jason came by for a visit, which was great and it got me up and at 'em! Not much to say, as I'm feeling crappy so I'm in grind mode.

Just a zombie going through the motions, preparing to start coming back. I'll do it but I've been doing it for a very long time. Need to recharge, which is what I'm doing. My head is clear—not worrying about anything but the task at hand. Again, I'm a lucky man.

Megan's Journal
December 22, 2008

I kept thinking—all day—how could I get to see you! You were snowbound. I was snowbound. My heart ached knowing how lonely you must have been.

Chad's Journal
December 22, 2008

Finished my muesli, which always gets me off to a good day. Getting ready to start my strength bands, but not sure if today is the day. Soon, though.

This day turned nasty very quickly due to some shooting pains in my kidney that became progressively worse as afternoon led to evening. Most pain I've ever been in!

Doctors though I was passing a kidney stone but went down for CT scan and it didn't pick up on anything.

They just kept feeding me morphine.

MEGAN'S JOURNAL

December 23, 2008

Snowed in again! Your text messages have been getting more scrambled. You said you have been in lots of pain and they don't know what it was. I have been feeling so helpless!

Chad's Journal
December 23, 2008

Struggling, but it's all part of the battle. They now think I could have shingles so I'm waiting for those results. In the meantime, I've been put in isolation and am on rigorous antibiotic meds that are really affecting my appetite. Puked my guts out this morning... Lame!

Good thing I'm not a writer cause this is some boring shit I'm putting down on these pages. Anyway Christmas is two days away and all I want for Christmas is for this pain to be gone.

Megan's Journal
December 24, 2008

For the past two years, you and I have woken up on Christmas morning together. I'm trying not to give it too much thought—I just want to get to you!!

Still snowing. I started shoveling early in the day, dug my car out, and went upstairs to wrap gifts for your family and mine. I looked outside and saw that my car was covered again! Mom and Dad were listening to the traffic reports and said the roads were way too bad out of New West.

All your friends were calling and texting, saying that they were on their way to see you, and here I was stuck. I cried while wrapping all the gifts for our families, I was so sad. I wanted to be with you so badly.

After dinner, Dad dropped his 'dish duties' and drove me out to see you. I was so happy in the car. I couldn't help thinking about how awful it would have been for you to spend a snowy night without your love, and how I would never have forgiven myself if something happened and we weren't together for Christmas.

I was so happy to see you. You weren't as dopey as you sounded on the phone, and it was nice to see you fall asleep comfortably.

Merry Christmas, my honey...

I hope you know how much you mean to me...That I love you, and I will love you for better or for worse and in sickness and in health—forever and ever.

You make my life better, you make it worthwhile and you make me laugh so hard I think one day you'll make me pee my pants.

xoxo

December 25, 2008

We texted first thing in the morning. I was so unhappy and felt so badly that I had left you to wake up on Christmas day alone. I am so sorry.

You texted me again at 10:00 a.m., saying you needed me. You haven't asked much of me, so I knew you were serious. You said you were anxious and didn't know what had been really going on for the past few days.

When I got there, you were so happy to see me. I could tell you were really unhappy (and maybe a little scared?). I felt so needed.

You weren't able to enjoy any of the baking that friends and family had dropped by, so naturally, being the empathetic girlfriend that I am, I decided to eat as many cookies, brownies, almond bark and peppermint chocolate thingys as I could.

Shortly afterwards, you felt a little more comfortable, so we opened gifts.

To my Wifey at Christmas,

You are beautiful, so funny, talented, positive, determined, driven, loving and full of life!

I'm so lucky cause it's Christmas everyday being with you. That's why December 25th is no more exciting than any other day...but maybe it's a day to make sure the people you love know that.

You make me happy and I can only hope I make you feel half as fantastic as I feel.

Merry Christmas Meggie

I Love You

Chad

Thank you is not enough, Chad. Thank you for my very sparkly diamond tennis bracelet. It's Christmas Day, we're in the hospital, and yet this princess is very, very happy.

Despite my excitement, I could tell you weren't right. I didn't know if it was the chemo that was making you so tired, but you looked awful, sitting hunched over in that chair because you couldn't lie down, having a hard time breathing. I felt sick watching you be sick.

Your dad came by with his generous gifts. You were so uncomfortable you couldn't even enjoy his visit. He stayed awhile, then left to pick up Jen and her family from the airport. I thought I would go back to Mom and Dad's for Christmas dinner, around the time your dad left, but I could tell you weren't ready for me to leave and so I stayed.

After lots of sitting up—and finally managing to lie down—I asked if you wanted me to say longer. You asked that I just wait for you to get more comfortable. I knew you needed me, and I knew I needed to be there. You must have been very sick (and worried) to ask me to stay. You have never asked me for anything.

I had a few tears in the hall that day, worried and helpless— why wouldn't this pass?

You fell asleep around 9:30 p.m., so I went home. I was slightly more at ease, knowing you could fall asleep after a tiresome day.

The first bite of real nutrition I had that Christmas was at 11:00 p.m., when I shoveled a warmed-up plate of Christmas dinner into my mouth. Even though my mom's face perked up with relief that I was home, I knew the second I walked in the door that I should have stayed with you.

"WHAT DO YOU MEAN YOU DON'T KNOW?"

Megan's Journal
December 26, 2008

You called me this morning and said, "This is the first day of my recovery."You sounded great.You sounded like you, and, as you said, you were "out of the fog'" after a few days of morphine.

I was so excited! You were back. We were going to go for a walk around the ward, have lunch and dinner together and not lie in bed. Come'n recovery!

I arrived around noon to see a few nurses surrounding you. You were hunched over the chair.The nurses said you had suddenly become very short of breath.

You couldn't lie down or get comfortable. No one seemed to know what was going on.

The nurses on the Bone Marrow Transplant (BMT) ward called the ICU team up.

It didn't take long for them to decide you needed to go down to the ICU. It was quick!The BMT nurse (the long-haired, nice one) asked if I needed help cleaning out your room. They asked that I do that because they weren't sure how long you'd be down there. I almost lost it right there. "What do you mean you don't know?"

This was a quick fix! You'd go down to ICU, they'd fix you, and you'd come back up! I was still asked to clean up your room. I started packing your things, once you had been wheeled down to the ICU, and I was sobbing. I sat on your bed for a while with my back to the door and just let the tears flow. Then I tried to collect myself, and to get the Christmas things and your clothes together.

Thinking I had collected myself enough to talk, I called Rebecca at work to explain that you had gone down to the ICU and I couldn't work that night. But I couldn't get out the words "my boyfriend" before I started weeping. Needless to say, she didn't ask me any questions and I didn't work. I tried to call Mom and Dad, but the line was busy, so I called Adrienne. I had a quick cry and once it was out, went back to cleaning the room.

I was so thankful that I didn't make eye contact with anyone on my three trips back and forth to the car. My heart knew this would be a quick ICU visit, but that dark part of my mind started thinking, "Is this what it's like to clean someone's room when they've passed away?" Awful thoughts. More tears.

When I was able to go see you in the ICU, you were all hooked up: masks, heart, IVs—the works. Although I'd only been gone an hour, I expected the nurse standing outside your room to tell me the good news. But although things had stabilized, there was no great news. You were pretty out of it.

That good-looking Dr. Sweet was great to you—both upstairs in BMT and down here. Doctors and nurses kept coming in to ask questions. I didn't know why I knew answers to your questions (Bowel movements? Weight? Urine? Breathing?), but I was so happy I was there. Who would have answered for you?

You dozed off. I stayed by your bed and read. Then I called your parents and told them the situation. (They were now snowed in too).

The next few hours are blurry to me. When I came back from calling your parents, I was told that, because it was 8:00pm, I wasn't allowed to visit you until the shift changed at 8:30—I almost raged. But when I did get back in, you were so happy to see me! You couldn't talk, but I could see it in your eyes—and your hand squeezed mine. I was happy I was back, too.

We chatted for a while. (I talked, you muttered.) Around 11:00 p.m. you started to fade, and by midnight you fell asleep. Because of the snow, and because I was worried, I slept in the reclining chair down the hall. I set my alarm for 2:30 a.m. so I could come in and see how you were doing. At 9:30 the next morning, I updated your parents (and mine) and helped you wash. You were much better. Everyone was pleased with how well you were responding to the heart medications. You would be back upstairs by tonight!

That being said, we weren't too eager to get upstairs. We liked the care in the ICU. Things were under control here.

They thought you might need a catheter, but you said no, so I helped you pee into a bucket that I had them bring. I love you so much that I didn't think twice about it. Crazy how gross things never seem gross in situations like that! I fed you soup, too. I think you were annoyed with me because I was feeding you too fast. Sorry, I was just excited you were eating.

Around 4:00 p.m., they were ready to take you back upstairs. Although I was hesitant (and maybe you were too?) that they might not be ready for you upstairs, we'd decided it would be okay.

I love you so much, it makes me cry.

Jen, Bill, your dad, Ben and Lauren came to visit. Seeing your family brought an instant feeling of relief to me, but perhaps I could have warned them about the state you were in.

Your sister and Bill were fine, but having the kids see you like that may not have been the best thing. I could only hope the excitement of Christmas has overwritten the disturbance of seeing their beloved Uncle Chad hooked up to machines and breathing through a mask like Darth Vader.

WHAT HAPPENED?

Megan's Journal
December 27, 2008

So now that we're out of the ICU, we've decided to ask lots of questions. Thank goodness we did. Once we got back up to the ward, your breathing immediately changed again. The ICU team was up there, nurses buzzing around making sure things were set up for you, and that awful bumbling nurse was hanging things. You were lying down on the bed, and you looked worried.

Trying to catch your breath and get more comfortable, you went and sat on the chair. There the nurse started hanging more stuff. You asked what it was for, and he just said he was giving you the same things they were giving you downstairs, but "they did things differently up here," so he was hooking things up accordingly. (Red flag #1)

When the nurse brought in the plastic patches for your heart, he looked at me and asked, "These are for smoking right?" Me: "Excuse me?" Him: "These are because he's a smoker, right?" Me: (Looked at you. Looked at the ICU doc.) "No! They are for his heart rate!" Him: "Uh, well…Megan, here's a pill that you can give him." Me: "What is it?" Him: "Uh, I don't know. Let me check." He came back with the chart. "I don't know what it is, but here's the name. I don't know how to say it."

I almost lost my mind. My whole body may have turned a shade of red. I was so upset and angry. Watching you struggle to breathe, with a nurse who didn't seem to know what he was doing, feeling like everything was going out of control. Thank goodness that the ICU doc was there.

I called Mom and Dad, and when they offered to drive in, I accepted. You and I really needed someone to help look after us. I was feeling so helpless, watching you be so uncomfortable, and in a blur from the past few days; I was trying to ask questions when I had no idea what the right or wrong answers were.

When they came in, Mom kissed you on your forehead. (Like her grandma and mom did to her, and she did to me. It's the way my mom lets you know she loves you.) You choked up a bit and I melted inside. It was then that I realized you weren't worried about letting them know how upset you were, emphasizing how bad you felt.

Mom took me for dinner. I was going on 48 hours at the hospital, and I hadn't gone out for air other than to take your things to the car. It was so nice to get out. Any other time I had been out of the hospital, I had always felt the pull to go back and make sure that everything is okay. I also felt guilty: you don't get a break, so why should I?

But I felt better knowing that Dad was with you, monitoring things while you rested. When I asked if it was okay if we all went out for dinner, you said it was okay, but when I asked if you wanted someone to stay, you nodded yes. Enough said.

You and Dad chatted, and when Mom and I came back to the room, you were both in the same position as when we had left.

Dad told us that you had lifted your Ativan pills in a "cheers," and he had asked the nurse to put in another request so you could have two. You started to get sleepy. Mom offered to stay, so I could go home, (she had even packed a night bag), but I felt refreshed after dinner and like things were more under control. I tucked myself back in to my chair-bed and waited until you fell asleep. You started snoring in about 15 minutes. Phew! I could finally go to sleep.

Every time you moved or went to the bathroom that night, I woke up. I was on such high alert. Around 2:30 a.m. you woke up and said you thought you might need the breathing tubes again. You went on the nose prongs and then, a few hours later, on a breathing mask. I asked the nurse to get those set up and to call for the ICU team as I could tell your breathing was becoming stressed again. Just before, I had heard a code blue called over the loudspeaker. I knew it was going to be awhile until they got up here.

I reemphasized to the nurse that she should call the ICU team and make sure they got up to the room soon. I wasn't sure what the time gap was, but I know you had another sleeping pill somewhere in there. The ICU team came up around 5:30 a.m. and decided you needed the breathing mask from the ICU. They started asking you questions about your breathing: when things became uncomfortable for you, and when did you have your last sleeping pill and all that. You were so dozy that you couldn't answer. I was so happy I had stayed the night and knew the answers. What would have happened if I hadn't been there?

The ICU team said that they would see how the rest of the night and morning went, and they could bring you back downstairs once a bed opened up.

You woke up around 8:00 a.m., and I heard the nurse talking to you. You asked, "What happened?" Apparently you had woken up in a panic and hadn't known why you had the mask on. I explained things to you, as you only seemed to hear what I said. He persuaded you to put the mask back on and you slept for a few more hours.

There were so many different breathing machines it was hard to keep track. There were the little dinky ones that attached under your nose, good to help regulate your breathing when it's hard for you to take deep breaths. Then there was the mask—it seemed like you get more oxygen throughout your body when you were on it than on the nose tubes. Then there was the ICU breathing mask—and that was more of an apparatus. It comes with a big machine on wheels that sits beside your bed. It has spiny things on it, and sounds so loud, like it is breathing for you. I'm sure I was told more about what it did, but with so much going through my mind, all I was capable of computing was: No breathing tubes: good. Little breathing tubes: okay. Breathing mask: Could be better. ICU breathing mask-machine: I'm pretty sure Darth Vader used it to survive, so it should do wonders for you. That shit was serious.

THE SICKEST PERSON ON

THE WARD

Megan's Journal
December 28, 2008

When you woke up, it was much harder for you to breath. The ICU team came back up to see how things were going. You had lots of fluids in your lungs. You couldn't get comfortable. The red-headed Irish doctor came in to explain what was going on with you.

She didn't have too many answers, just that your heart was having the same problem that it was the day before. Dr. Sweet came in to see you as well. He was so good. They didn't think you had a heart attack, but they didn't know what was causing this floppy heart. But what they did know was that they needed to get you downstairs so they could figure out what was going on.

My heart started racing. I was panicking because it was so hard for you to talk and I knew so little about what was going on. Between breaths, you asked me if I could ask for an Ativan to try and make you more comfortable. I found the Irish doctor and asked for one, and she told me that they had to be very careful what they gave you. She said that your heart was very weak, and that an Ativan could disguise what was really going on. She went on to tell me that they were "very, very worried about you and that you are the sickest person on the ward right now."

(*But hey!* We are on the freakin' BMT ward, lady! Everyone is sick.)

It was after that comment that I felt myself crumble. I went back in to see you, and to explain why you couldn't have the Ativan you wanted. From the way you looked at me, I think you could tell I knew something.

You looked up at me with your yellow eyes and breathed, "What do you think of this?"

I said that I thought you needed to go to the ICU. Choking back tears, I stepped out to call Mom and Dad.

I called and I couldn't talk. Dad just kept saying, "Talk to me." I could barely get anything out. He and Mom were on their way. I asked him what I should tell your parents, because I had promised them I would call in the morning with an update. How do I make a call like that?? Dad said to hold off until he got there and we knew more.

I went back into the room, and you were slipping in and out of consciousness.

"I don't know how long I can do this," you huffed.

Oh, my god, what is happening?

I just sat with you and petted you, facing away so you couldn't see my tears, unseeingly flipping through a magazine while we waited for someone to come in with more news.

My mom and dad walked into the room. I gave them the run down before losing it with Mom in the hall. I didn't even make it past the nurses' station before I started weeping. I couldn't catch my breath. Mom is a crier, but she went into emergency mode and was so strong for me. Not a tear! I told her what the nurses and doctors had said, and how awful you looked, and how the whites of your eyes were now yellow.

I couldn't get it together, and couldn't help sobbing. "Is this it?? Am I really watching the end happening?" After I got it all out and Mom's calm voice and reassurance helped me clear my mind, we went back in to see you. You were less and less aware of what was going on. At some point, the doctors suggested that, when you went down to the ICU, they might have to intubate you. You asked Dad what he thought.

"It's not too bad, and that way they can have control over what's going on in your body," Dad explained calmly.

At this point, they were getting ready to take you downstairs. We got your things, and I came with you. Reminding us that we couldn't go in while you were getting 'set up,' Dad suggested that Mom and I should leave for a while.

We came back a few hours later (at some point I called your parents and told them—without crying —what was going on and that my parents were there, too.) Your dad came in, and I was able to see you in the ICU. You looked better: more comfortable, with less heaving.

After going through everything that had happened with our parents, I went home with Mom and Dad. I knew you would be better after a goodnight's sleep.

NOT VERY MANY

PEOPLE SURVIVE.

Megan's Journal
December 29, 2008

Today was one of the worst days.

After spending a few days in the ICU, you were doing pretty good! You were breathing using only the nose prongs. You were able to drink a little bit and eat a little bit too.

It was around 4:00 p.m. that you started to feel short of breath again, and asked if you could put the breathing mask back on. Once it was on, you tried to get your breathing rhythm back, and soon after, the head of the ICU came in.

He assessed you, asking you a few of the questions that everyone else had been asking, and then sat down on the chair beside the bed. He started explaining what your heart was doing and what the medications you were on were doing. My first thought was, "This guy is good! He is explaining things so thoroughly."

"Well, Chad, I've got two questions that I'm asking right now," he continued. "One, what caused your heart to do this? And two, what are we going to do about it?"

He paused in his real doctor-posture way. "I don't know the answer to the first question, but I do know that we are going to try and fix this problem with a combination of drugs. If that doesn't work, we'll try another combination."

I would have liked him to stop there, but he didn't. "I do have to tell you, Chad, that if these different options don't work, this is very serious. We may have to put you on life support." You nodded with the mask on your face. "And I have to tell you, this is a very serious decision. If it gets to that point, to be honest, not very many people survive."

You nodded again. "We are going to do everything we can for you, okay?" He stood up from his chair, looked at the many beeping, monitoring machines behind you and then reached over to clumsily re-button your robe.

He reached over and shook your hand, looked at me and left.

As soon as he left, my eyes filled with tears. How could he? How could he? How could he give you that information while you were fighting to breath on a machine!? You saw that I was upset and said that it was okay, you just wanted to try and get some sleep.

I left the room and cried.

Later, when we talked about what the doctor had said, you felt it was good there was a plan. Your mind is so strong and clear—you are wonderful.

I ALMOST LOOK LIKE ME!

Megan's Journal
December 30, 2008

When I walked in this morning, you were sleeping contently. There was much more color in your face.

Knowing how precious your sleep is, I went across the street to Starbucks.

I called Katharine and we talked for a while. I didn't expect to ever find myself in a situation where calling your first love for advice seemed like a good idea, but I explained to her that I needed to talk to someone who had seen you rebound, someone who had witnessed your comebacks. I am looking for a light at the end of the tunnel and I can't see anything. I needed to hear that you were going to be okay.

She recalled how you'd heard the worst news possible, and how everything could change for the better in just a few minutes. No matter what bad news you've had, she went on, no matter how sick you've been, you've fought through and recovered. Seven years later, you're fighting again, and you will get through it.

My phone died in the middle of our conversation, but I had heard enough to make me feel better. When I came back to your room, you were sitting up in bed looking (relatively) lively. While I was out, a nurse had come in and shaved your head, so the patchy spots where your hair had been falling out were gone. You looked sooo good! You had lost so much of the fluid in your face and the rest of your body that I felt like I was looking at Chad again.

I took a picture of you and showed you. You were pleased with what you saw.

"I almost look like me!"

We spent the rest of the afternoon looking through pictures of you from the past year or two, talking about how well and unwell you have been. We talked about your recovery: what we want to do together and what we had to look forward to. This made me so happy, but you also warned me that you've been disappointed too many times and need to take things one day at a time.

So today we started doing your exercises. I tried to think of the simplest moves that would help your body get moving again. We started slow, with 10 leg raises while sitting on the bed, 10 stand-ups from a chair, and 10 arm raises while sitting. I knew that even these minor movements were hard for you, but we are going to do them every day. No matter what. We are going to get you stronger!

I left the hospital feeling so good. I felt you were on your way up and out of there.

January 1, 2009

It's the New Year! Happy 2009!

Here's what's been happening for you over the past few days.

Every three days, something has improved. Your leg raises, stand-ups and arm raises get easier. You've been moved to the cardiac care unit. It is quiet and dark, but you said you like the way they take care of you.

The first day I came to see you there, you looked up and saw me and said, "Ah, you found me! I'm so happy you found me! I was so lonely. I didn't think you would come!" I loved that. I felt needed and appreciated. I love you so much. I am so happy I can help you through this!

Then you developed a pain in your side and started peeing blood. I got nervous again. Three more days went by and it wasn't getting better. When I visited, you were groggy and in pain. You dozed off every once in a while and would ask me to help adjust pillows and get you things. Pass you this and clean up that.

For the first time since you were admitted, when I left you, I felt pissed off. I was angry that although you have dozens of qualified, caring nurses around you, when I arrive after working all day, you ask me to do everything for you. It was like you wanted to relieve the nurses of caring for you.

Then I got even more angry with myself for being angry in the first place. You didn't choose this. You didn't get to rest, so why should I?

I just needed some sleep.

I'M READY TO GO HOME.

Megan's Journal
January 7, 2009

On Wednesday night, you had just finished asking me to help adjust things before I left. I was tired and ready to leave, and you asked me to help clean up your room and put things in your bag.

I need you to be better soon! I'm tired of being tired and I'm tired of you being sick!! I felt badly for being upset—not with you, but the situation.

Then I had to give my head a shake. I shouldn't have been so selfish in thinking that I wanted a break.

You were getting better each day for a while, and now there is nothing again. Nothing was getting better and we were at a stand-still. I felt like the light at the end of the tunnel was dimming and the fog was settling in again.

I am so emotionally fatigued. I feel so badly, being the lucky one that gets to go home every night, get up and go to the gym while you don't get a break from this. I wish I could do something to make this easier on you.

You spent a few more days in the cardiac unit, and then headed back upstairs to the BMT ward. My mom arrived in time to help you move up. Afterward, she said that when you came up to your new room, she saw your color change immediately. You hadn't seen daylight in a week!

Chad's Journal
January 9, 2009

Ooops. Had some setbacks.

Body was overloaded, passed a kidney stone, went into heart failure, pissing knives and blood....good times.

Things are improving slowly. I need to be aware, patient and positive! Started walking today, which is a good start. Appetite is pretty good, but I'm still dealing with this bladder pain. Anyway, must keep rolling along—good days and bad!

Excited to begin healing and hoping my counts go up. They have been giving me daily injections that seem to be working to help boost my counts. Had some great visits from people the last couple of days but talking does tire me out right now.

Megan's mom, Brenda, showed up at the perfect time to help me move upstairs yesterday. So sweet. Then she left me food for a couple days, and puffed wheat squares—which I love!

January 12, 2009

Since I've come back to the BMT ward, things have improved. I'm still having a hard time with my bladder. Blood clots and lots of blood.

I'm walking four or five times each day, just doing laps of the ward.

Anyway, I'm ready to go home soon but I'm not convinced my body is ready yet.

Nap time!

Megan's Journal
January 17, 2009

Yea!!! Today was your first full day at home.

It was so hard for both of us. All night I woke up at any change in your breathing or any noise out of your mouth. I was really hoping that sleeping in your own bed would help you get a good night sleep. Boy, was I wrong!

When we woke up, you had soaked the bed with an early-morning fever.

Though you are out of the hospital, you'll be going in daily to the outpatient clinic. After dropping you off this morning, I hoped to slip out and see my parents, but no such luck. Why do you keep asking for things? Your nurse is right there! I'm not your nurse! I know you need me, and I know you wouldn't be asking me to stay if you didn't need me. If there were anything you could do for yourself, you would be doing it. I'm sorry. I'm just tired.

I am so tired of this. I feel sorry for myself. I feel lonely, and like I have no one to take care of me. (Even writing this, I feel embarrassed.)

I decided to settle in for the long haul and sat in the reclining chair beside you. "I like seeing you happy," you said. It reminded me how much my mood affects you, and how I need to stay positive. Promising myself I wouldn't let you see anymore of my downer attitudes, I drifted off into a deep sleep.

Once we got home, you asked me to hang your jacket and if there were any pillows. The only pillows we have are right there! About 30 seconds later, you said you were sorry.

Tonight I walked into the bedroom to see you sitting on the side of the bed, crying. You said you were so scared by how weak you were and how badly you felt. I tried to say something comforting, something positive, but whatever came out didn't seem to make a difference.

Goodnight, Chaddy. I am happy you are home. I hope you (we) have a better sleep tonight. Everything is better in the morning.

I love you.

January 19, 2009

Dear Chaddy,

Day three at home. You slept like you had been knocked over the head. I had to feel your breath again and again to make sure you were alive! (Just kidding, but seriously.)

I was so happy you had a good sleep. You woke up this morning and made yourself breakfast. (Yeah!)

I went to work and you went to the clinic. You drove yourself today, but later declared it may have been a bit premature as you were carsick and tired for the rest of the day.

We discussed what might happen when you have your next bone marrow biopsy. You said you were nervous, but trying to focus on the positive. I wished I could always think like you. I have to try harder to take things one day at a time, because the idea of getting a bone marrow biopsy and not hearing the results we want to hear is devastating. What if all this was for nothing? What would we do?

You just came to bed, and I'm so happy you're home. I love you so much, and I hope we never have to sleep apart again (excluding weekend girl trips, of course).

I love you with all my heart.

Forever and ever,

M

January 20, 2009

Dear Chad,

Today was a better day for you again. I think that the better you sleep and the more you get used to home, the stronger you are.

They found a small infection around your lungs. That's why you were having pain. Weird to say, but that was good news. At least they have figured out what has been giving you pain and how to fix it.

You sat up and walked around the apartment for the whole time I was home tonight. I admire how much you push yourself to be stronger.

We watched Barack Obama's inauguration tonight, and when Garth Brooks performed, you danced with me. Even when you are feeling as poor as you do, you are still romantic. I love you so much.

Goodnight. Xo

January 21, 2009

Dear Chad,

I haven't seen many of your friends this past month, so when Corey was over tonight, I was keen to catch up. I could see you were tired, but I was also trying to be polite.

"You just don't stop fucking gabbing," you said after he left. "It's painful."

Although I feel sorry for your couch-bound self, I hope you stop saying things like this when you feel better. Please don't take your fatigue out on me.

But, since you're asking, I'll join you for snuggles now.

I love you. Even though you frustrate me. I love you through it all.

M

January 25, 2009

Dear Chad,

Your second weekend at home!

Last week you couldn't climb a flight of stairs without needing to stop for a rest. Now you can climb eight flights of stairs and walk up hills. Today you went for a walk with your dad. I am so proud of you!

Tonight you told me how happy you were to be here with me, because there was a while in the hospital when you didn't think you were going to make it.

I wondered what you were thinking then, and hearing it now makes my throat ache, remembering how awful it all was.

Okay, you are trying to feel me up right now, so I'll finish and continue writing tomorrow.

As always, I love you. Goodnight.

M

January 26, 2009

Chaddy,

I love you more and more every day.

Sometimes I find myself looking at you thinking, "How lucky I am to spend a lifetime laughing with this man." xoxo

January 27, 2009

Hallo sleeping bear!

You finally went to see a urologist today. I have lost count of how many weeks you have been peeing blood.

They have made you lay off acidic foods to see if that helps.

You are also on an antibiotic that gave you some kind of reaction. I think you worried you were having a heart attack. As I folded laundry tonight, I thought about how uncomfortable and awful it must be to be in your body. You can't escape it.

Tonight you apologized for how bad you've been feeling. I never want you to feel bad for not being able to help out or not having energy for me. I mean really... in the span of our lifetime together, we are just going to look back and say, "That was a tough time, but—glad we're through it!" And we'll be living happily ever after · and you'll be cooking, cleaning and taking care of me!

Rest up my love—a lifetime is a very long time :)
Xo M

A DATE!

Megan's Journal
February 6, 2009

We talked earlier about maybe going out for dinner or a movie tonight, and I got so excited at the idea. For the first time in over two months, we were going on a date!

But when I came home, I could tell by how you were feeling that date night would be delayed. That was okay. I was also pretty tired and was really just looking forward to spending time with you.

Then my co-worker texted, inviting us to join her and her husband for drinks. I had a sharp pang, wishing we could. But here we were, Friday night, grumbling at each other.

I hope that we'll be back doing fun social things as a couple again one day.

And I know all of this sounds selfish, but I know you want it too. I know you are working as hard as you are so we can have that. I hope we get better soon.

Anyway, *the great news is* that your heart is now pumping at 50% capacity!!! A big jump from the 20% it was at while in the ICU.

And in other great news, you've been asked to speak at a press conference with Diana Krall, Elvis Costello, Dr. Nantal and Diana's sister, Michelle. Diana and Michelle lost their mom to multiple myeloma and, like you, they are fundraising for the VGH and UBC Hospital Foundation. The press conference is a prelude to their *very* fancy gala, where Elton John, James Taylor and Sarah McLaughlin will be performing.

I can't tell you how proud I am that you will be speaking on behalf of the patients battling the disease.

I know how grateful you are for everything that the doctors and nurses and the rest of your care team have done for you, and how much you want to express that gratitude by raising money for research. I somehow feel that, for you, this is the real start to that campaign.

I also can't tell you how excited I am that we have been invited to the gala.

THE PLAN

Chad's Journal
February 2009

2009 Goals + Objectives

Clean recovery from Transplant #2
Reach fundraising goal of $1M
Continue with stock investment plan (next 60%)
Work on being more balanced person; less reactive, more proactive

How:

Confidence
Positivity
Happiness
Consistency
Love
Hard work
Focus

Travel for 2009/2010

Europe June 2009
Australia March 2010
Asia/South Africa March/April 2010

Megan

Love
Let her do + be Meg
Control anger
Long and happy relationship!

I CAN'T DO THAT TO MY

GIRLFRIEND.

That spring was so long. There was no longer a distinction between boyfriend-girlfriend and patient-caregiver. We argued.

The only role Chad had room for in his life was Warrior. He was focused solely on his recovery. Consequently, the roles I adopted were caretaker, supporter and pain-in-his-ass.

I watched him with admiration. If we crossed paths during lunch hour, I'd see him working out with the elastic exercise bands, careful not to lose his form and not to overextend himself. Other days he would be following the downward dog instructions on his Power Yoga with Rodney Yee DVD.

Some evenings I joined him in walking flights of stairs in our apartment building. Sometimes I was so fed up with walking those stairs with him, trying not to talk so he could focus. When I did join him, I didn't feel good. When I didn't join him, I felt even worse.

As Chad grew stronger, I grew weaker—not physically, but mentally. Chad had never really gone into detail about why he and

Katherine broke up, but I was starting to understand what might have happened. This relationship was hard.

The universe seems to find a way to test us in these periods of weakness, and my heart and relationship were vulnerable.

One afternoon, the past reappeared on my smartphone.

Sender: Rookie

I could hear his clever voice through his flattering texts. I was filled with guilt each time I returned his message.

Over the course of the next few weeks, our messages were frequent, and I looked forward to them.

I made sure to tell him I lived with my boyfriend, hoping that, by saying so, I somehow justified messaging with another guy.

I told Chad as well, mentioning how cool it was that one of my college friends now played for a major league baseball team.

Then my moral boundaries were tested further as a few girl-friends decided on a girls' trip to New York City in April.

"It should be fun. He said he'll be able to put aside tickets for us," I said to Chad as we lay in bed, just after my phone had lit up with a text from Rookie. Without looking at me, Chad noncha-lantly asked, "How often do you talk to him?"

My stomach turned with remorse, wishing the answer wasn't "every few days."

"Why do you ask?"

"No reason. Just wondering."

That's it? He's not bothered I'm talking to another guy?

A few days later, I was on a flight to New York, where I met with Kelli, Lena and Camilla for a weekend that all of us seemed to need. At 24, each of us was in some kind of life transition. It was comforting to be together, uncertainly attempting to describe what we were doing with our lives.

On game day, the sun was out, the beer tasted good, and two hot dogs didn't feel like enough. Three of us had been friends with Rookie in Jacksonville, and we talked about how impressive it was to see his name on the Jumbotron. The glitz and glamour of temptation shone right in my eyes all afternoon.

After the game, we weaseled our way down to the friends and family area, where I would see Rookie for the first time since college.

He was handsome, and we couldn't prevent the warm smiles we gave each other when our eyes met.

But later he didn't meet us for dinner as he'd planned. Instead, he sent me a text: "I don't trust myself around you, and I can't do that to my girlfriend."

I read his text five times. Then I read it to my loyal friends. And then I burst into tears of simultaneous relief and disappointment.

I was so relieved that I was no longer in a situation that threatened my commitment to Chad. And I was so disappointed I hadn't been the one to stop it. The flattery and attention I had been drawn to was over.

And I was forced to take a hard look at what my relationship with Chad had become.

CHAD'S JOURNAL

April 2009

I must admit, I'm eager to get through this particular part and on to some other things. My second transplant was a dreadful time in my life, from which I'm still recovering. I said to Megan a few weeks back that I really hadn't recovered from the first transplant when we started preparing; anytime I'd start to recover, I'd get hit again, and that's just the way it's gone.

It's taken every last ounce of physical, mental and emotional energy I had in me. For the first time in nine years, I was broken.

For years I'd managed to putt along...knowing I was getting worse, but never really feeling too worried...living in the moment.

In the summer of 2008, desperation entered my life. I'd reached the point that had always haunted me somewhere at the back of my mind. I was running out of options. I'd had every myeloma treatment available to me, and now the well was running dry.

The doctor I saw at the Mayo Clinic is one of the leading myeloma specialists in the world, and she was so cool to me. After an hour-long consultation, she agreed my best chance for a better life would be a second transplant.

The next step was finding my original donor, who agreed to donate again. Some people never find a donor, and I'm lucky enough to get one who was willing to do it twice...I have no words!

The transplant itself was as anticlimactic as the first. It only took about a half hour for the marrow to drip in. I felt so relieved, and was full of emotion and anxiety, which soon came pouring out on Meg's shoulder.

Afterward, I was a train wreck. But after six weeks I stumbled my way out to the fresh air and to Megan waiting by the curb... whewwww!

WALK IT OFF.

"Be there in 2 mins"

I was waiting outside the international arrivals platform and, as expected, Chad would not only be there at 2:00 a.m. sharp to pick me up but had texted me to confirm his arrival.

I ignored the honk from the guy in black Audi convertible as I kept my eager eyes peeled for Chad in his green Jeep.

"Meg!" yelled the guy in a hoodie from the black convertible.

Holy Shit! Chad?! What the...

Grinning at me with a "What? So I got an awesome new car while you were gone," smirk on his face, he slipped the car into park, walked around the back and lifted my bag into the trunk.

When he leaned in for a quick kiss, I was hit with an enormous amount of relief that I was home.

I slid into the heated, black leather seat so comfortably I swore I was meant to be his leading lady in the scene of an Italian car ride romance.

"You liiikeee it?" He looked across at me from under his hoodie.

As he showed off the tight-turning craftsmanship of the Audi TT's features, Chad explained that he was just in for a casual look at the dealership down the street that day when this little flashy soft-top caught his eye. "It will be a fun little thing for us to whip around in for the summer," he justified.

Gone were the days of the practical Jeep, and here were the zippy, carefree days of summer. I could see how he felt behind the wheel when the gears would shift from fast to faster; for those moments in his medicated and structured day, Chad had regained control.

We were getting close to the 100-day mark, post-transplant, and the improvements in his health were starting to show. His skin had lost the grey of early recovery and had recovered its pinkish hue. His shoulders had broadened with muscle from his careful light-weight routine, and his waist had filled out again thanks to regaining his appetite.

But while Chad was reestablishing his control during the days, our nights were often the opposite. I'd awaken as he lurched uncontrollably out of bed with cramping hamstrings, quads and calves (often all at once), a result of the permanent neuropathy he had acquired from various drugs.

As he waddled and rocked around our living room, he'd lean on me, trying to release the tightness. Some nights it would be 20 minutes before he managed to sit down and gulp down the Vitamin C water, Powerade and banana that helped bring some relief. While he moaned in tired agony, I'd rub his legs to help get the circulation back. Sometimes this worked, and we'd go back to bed. But many times he'd shoot back up from the couch moaning, "They won't fucking release!"

I was never able to get used to the sharpness of his attitude when this happened, though I did learn to understand that it was never meant for me. And like Chad with his cramps, I just needed to be patient and walk it off.

I DON'T HAVE TO DRESS UP, DO I?

Date: 3:38 PM Thursday, May 21, 2009

From: Megan

To: Laura, Uros, Matt, Diana, Bryn, Concetta, Adrienne, Todd, Vanessa, Sharon, Jason, Karen, Corey

Subject: Surprise for Chad

Hey gang,

So by suggestion of Diana, and some teasing from Chad about not having done anything for his birthday back in February (he has no idea that you were all lined up and ready to celebrate then—I never told him), we have decided to throw him a VERY belated surprise birthday party. (It could just be called a 'hey, let's all get together' thing, but I figure the guy has worked so hard to get where he is that he could use a little shindig in his name. And this time he will be able to enjoy it.

Suggest to anyone you think would like to come, or who Chad would like to have there. Just please don't tell him.

xox M

Getting his 30 closest supporters there was not a problem. Getting Chad there took some convincing.

Unless the menu had chicken fingers, hot wings, or he could wear his flip-flops and hoodie, "dinner out" wasn't something he was too interested in.

Jesse, Adrienne, Bryn and I pitched the idea of a casual dinner out. Chad's poker friends arranged the desserts and balloons. All we had to do was get him there.

"Where the hell are we going, anyway? I don't have to dress up, do I?"

Chad still had a cord plugged into his chest for blood and platelet transfusions, and was unconcerned if it poked out of his earth-toned Banana Republic v-necks.

"I don't care what you wear."

I totally care.

The restaurant had a strict no flip-flop or baseball hat rule, and I was a bit panicked that Chad wouldn't be allowed into his own party.

While Jesse and Adrienne kept Chad occupied, I quietly spoke to the hostess from my cell in the bedroom and warned, "Uh...so the birthday boy wants to wear flip flops."

"No problem," she said, chuckling. Crisis averted.

"SUUURRRPPPPRRRIIIISSSEEEE!!!!!"

Everyone was sitting and standing around a room filled with helium balloons, streamers and party hats.

"Uhhhh..." He was baffled.

I rushed my explanation, trying to get it all in before people started coming up to him. "Surprise? Happy belated birthday! We tried to plan this for your real birthday and then again for your 100 days, but we wanted you to be able to enjoy it. So... Surprise?"

I didn't see much of him for the rest of the night. Flip-flopping his way around the room, whenever I looked over Chad was either wrapped up in man hugs, laughing with his head thrown back or playing with his new toy gifts. It was his first real night back to the world.

I READ SOME OF YOUR
JOURNAL THIS MORNING.

My desk at work faced away from the back door, but it was easy to recognize the familiar rumble of Chad's car pulling into the parking lot.

"Come outside," he texted.

The unexpectedness of the visit made me shoot up from my desk. Walking into the heat of the midday sun, I saw Chad reach down to grab a large, fragrant-looking bouquet from the passenger seat.

"What is this for?!"

We had quarreled the night before, after he said, "You just don't understand what this has been like."

"You know what!? You're right. I don't understand what you've been through." I picked up my navy, letter-filled journal from my bedside drawer and waved it at him. "But you don't understand what it's been like for me! Don't forget that I've been through this, too, and when you're ready, take a look at these letters. They're for you."

He was quick to respond, "I'm not going to read those."

When I saw the bouquet, I knew he'd heard what I had said last night.

"I'm really sorry, Meg. I don't know if I should have or not, but I read some of your journal. I couldn't get through them all. It was too painful, knowing I put you through that."

His sincerity made me feel badly. I never meant for that journal to make him feel guilty.

"Anyways, I'm just really sorry. These are for you, and you deserve far more than this. I'm off to clinic now, but just read the card, and I'll see you at home later."

I'm sorry. I read some of your journal this morning. You were right. I need to read it, as it opened my mind. I've been so selfish, focusing on getting better myself, forgetting you are also healing.

What you endured is my worst nightmare. The thought of losing you makes me ill. You have been there for me wholeheartedly and it's time for me to do the same for you. I said some horrible things to you, only because I'm scared to lose you, and it's my way of protecting myself. You are one of a kind, Megan Williams, and I promise to work hard to give you everything you desire.

I love you forever, Chad.

HERE WE GO, HONEY.

The thought of Chad missing another family wedding upset me so much that I ignored the possibility of it altogether. Even though my ticket to England had been booked for months, the trip wouldn't feel certain until Chad was given the medical go-ahead to leave the country with us.

The wedding was three weeks away, and it was still "too soon" to tell if his doctors would allow him to travel.

"*Dad*!!! Chad can come!!!" I called the second I heard Chad got the green light from Dr. Nantal. His care-team decided that they could give him 10 days away.

"Shit…that's bloody fantastic. I knew he'd make it." The relief in Dad's voice was obvious.

Plans were quickly put in motion to make this the bucket-list trip Chad had been pushing to get healthy enough for: London, Amsterdam and Paris in 10 days.

"Here we go, honey…" I squeezed Chad's hand as we stepped from the loading dock onto the plane. It was as if packing, checking in and customs still wasn't enough to convince him that he had made it.

Once on the plane, he sat down and organized his gigantic Toblerone bar and Men's Health Magazine, and acquainted himself with the TV system, yet he still looked unsettled.

It wasn't until the flight attendant announced the plane's doors were closed that I saw Chad give a deep exhale and allow his shoulders to relax.

Getting on this flight and getting to Europe had been such a lifelong goal, and such a long shot at the same time—to watch Chad realize that he had done it was one of my life's most powerful, gratifying moments.

ANOTHER BUCKET LIST ITEM.

Meeting my family for the first time, Chad finally came face-to-face with the silent fighters who had been supporting him from a distance for so long. They knew what an accomplishment it was for him be alive, let alone get to England, and they embraced him accordingly.

The night of the wedding, we all drank celebratory champagne as though it was flowing from the taps. Except Chad, who nursed only a few drinks through the entire event.

The next morning, bright and early, Chad woke up to his alarm.

Alarm? The day after a wedding?!

He said he was heading to the racetrack, a place nearby where you could drive Ferraris, Audi R8's, and any other luxury car of your dreams. Say no more. Chad would get to that track.

Under grey clouds on the rain-splashed roads of a World War II airfield, Dad and I sloshed through muddy gravel following Chad's enthusiastic, boy-like stride.

Hazy-headed and less than excited to stand in the long line for an expensive experience, I didn't understand the appeal of this ordeal. That is, not until Chad took a Lamborghini around the track. Another bucket list item—check!

Next up, a few speedy laps in an Audi R8—check!

The rest of our holiday continued with the same momentum. Every window of energy was dedicated to the opportunity to do something neither of us had done before. We planed, trained, walked and taxied our way through London, Amsterdam and Paris, feeling more carefree than we'd ever been.

Over the month before, Chad and I had fallen in love all over again, and being away together compounded the intensity of our feelings for each other.

As we explored the cobblestone streets and cafés of Amsterdam, I regularly asked if he needed a rest. But each time I asked, I was met with the same response: "Nope, I'm all good." Chad was better.

We had three days in Paris together before he needed to be home to get 'juiced up' again. Unfortunately, not even the sparkling lights of the Eiffel Tower could keep Chad's energy from fading.

"I think I should just lay down," he said after a morning attempt to fuel his body with a "jambon et fromage" crepe at the foot of the Eiffel Tower.

All too familiar with Chad's low energy, I couldn't help but feel disappointed. Our last day in Paris and you want to go to the hotel?! I tried to adjust my thinking: it was not "want" to go back, it was "need" to go back.

He sighed with relief as he lay down on the creaky bed in our tiny Parisian room.

"If you think you're going to nap for a little while, I think I'll maybe get some shopping in." I felt the pressure between us release as I skipped down the winding staircase to the street. (Elevator? Paris? Non.)

We reconnected later with renewed energy. The bags under his eyes were gone, and the bags under my arms were stuffed with new purchases.

We bid au revoir in Paris—parting ways at Gare du Nord. Chad flew home, and I took the train back to London to spend a few more days with my family. We had shared the trip of a lifetime.

And by the time I returned to Vancouver, Chad would be rested and replenished with enough blood and fluids to reminisce about it.

CONGRATULATIONS!

"UNCLEEE CHHHHAAADDDDDDD!!!!"

It was a water fight for the ages. Chad's sister Jen, her husband Bill, and their kids, Lauren and Ben, were in Vancouver for their annual summer holidays. This year, two factors made their vacation different from their other recent visits: It was smokin' hot outside, and Uncle Chad was healthy enough to play with them—for hours.

I knew it was only one afternoon of an entire summer, but this water fight was a big deal for everyone sharing the spray. Chad was able to be the uncle he wanted to be, tearing around the beach with his niece and nephew, not sitting on the sidelines, wishing he had the energy to join in.

The perfect summer days continued through August. We'd been to Texas for another wedding and spent several weekends in the Okanagan.

We both enjoyed the strength that gaining 25 pounds of muscle had given him.

Chad sold his little Audi TT and upgraded to a swanky Audi S4. He was so proud of the sale and subsequent purchase that he brainstormed the possibility of launching a business buying and selling cars for people who didn't have the time to do the research.

We spent many hours zipping around in that car—solving life's great mysteries, listening to CD mixes, taking the long way to our destinations so our conversations could continue.

Over the years we had talked about "when we were married." Knowing that we would be together forever, "when" we got married never seemed that important.

But this summer was the first time Chad was well enough, for long enough, that we could wrap our heads around "forever together." Sitting at a stop light one Saturday afternoon, Chad said something that melted my heart. "I will never love you more than I do at this moment. I will never be more committed to you and to our life together than I am right now—and there is nothing I could ever say in front of a group of people that would make that more true than it is today.

"So when we decide to get married, let's do it when we want to have a big party and celebrate. Not because it is something we feel we should do."

I literally could not compute all that romance at one time, so all I did was reach over and run my fingers over his buzzed scalp and reply, "I agree."

All I had ever really wanted for our relationship was for there to be such an abundance of health that we could do anything we wanted to do—and that is what I had. At that moment, as the traffic light turned green, I had everything I had asked the universe for.

This little life of ours was about maximizing the time we had together, making up for the time that had been lost. It was about living the life that we wanted, doing what we were able to with what we had.

One evening, Chad took me for spin over the Lions Gate Bridge to pick up our friends Jesse and Adrienne. It was a hot August evening and a patio night was in order.

We tucked ourselves into a corner of the Boathouse—two Caesars, two beers. Jesse and Adrienne exchanged a glance when Chad uncharacteristically ordered his Corona. Tonight deserved a beer; we were celebrating.

During those dark winter nights, sleeping in the hospital chairs, waking up to the sound of Chad moaning and pacing the apartment in pain, I had dreamt of a day like this.

"So..." I started off once our drinks were set on the brewery-sponsored coasters, "Chad got some good news today." It was taking so much control to wait for him to say something.

"Ah yeah..." he said, with his typical discretion when sharing any kind of news about his health. "So my blood work came back today, and it showed that I'm cancer free."

Adrienne gasped and clapped her hands together, "Ohmigod. *Ohmigod*! Holy shit! Congratulations!!"

Jesse's face lit up with a brilliant smile as we clinked our glasses together.

The reality that there is no cure for multiple myeloma didn't change the fact that Chad's "cancer proteins" were suppressed beyond recognition. This was the closest thing we could get to remission. As the sunset turned the blue sky into shades of pink, I was overwhelmed with bliss, gratitude and triumph.

A LITTLE CHANGE.

"A nap?" I looked at him like he had five noses. "You haven't had one of those in awhile."

Obviously it's nothing. It had just caught me a little off guard, coming home from work, expecting to hear about another one of his routine days.

"Yeah, I must have just pushed myself a little hard at the gym today, that's all."

See? No other explanation necessary.

I might have forgotten Chad's report of the midday nap altogether, had he not had another one the following day.

"What?" I don't understand. "It's probably all the early mornings. The workouts and tennis are just catching up with you. Take a day off and let your body relax, ok?"

"Yeah, you're right. We're seeing Dr. Nantal soon, so I'll see if anything is up."

I heard what he said, but chose to dismiss the absurdity of his comment. Puh-lease, let's not think something 'is up' because you've had two naps in a row. I diagnosed the churning feeling in my stomach as hunger.

Chad and his parents picked me up from work and we drove to VGH together. For the first time, the four of us would be gathered there for reasons other than illness.

We were having a photo shoot for a cover story on the fundraising Chad and his parents had started working on for Hematology Research and Clinical Trials Unit. The photographer snapped dozen of frames, capturing different combinations of us together: Chad and I; Chad and his mom, Sandy; Chad and his dad, Clark; Sandy and Megan; Chad, Sandy and Dr. Nantal; Sandy and Dr. Nantal; Chad and Dr. Nantal.

However, when Chad and Dr. Nantal stood next to each other, they weren't laughing and sharing their typical questionable-taste bedside humor, as they tended to do. Their conversation was clearly a serious one-on-one.

My gut knew what my mind had chosen to ignore.

"He's noticed a little change in my blood work," Chad told me afterward. "I knew this wasn't going to last forever. I'll find out more next week when I go in for my appointment."

The 'little change' in his blood work prompted another bone marrow biopsy.

After a week of waiting, Chad was finally about to get his biopsy results. Neither of us slept well the night before, and we'd woken up early. We tried our best to carry on a 'regular' conversation before we started on our daily routine.

"Want to see a movie tonight?"

"Sure, sounds good. I'll look at what's playing."

The fall colors were vivid in the sun that day.

He looked healthy. Maybe it was the brightness of the day, or that a week of worry was about to be put to rest. No matter what the biopsy said, he certainly did not look sick.

My boss was always sensitive about making sure my home life was protected from office chatter, but that day she happened to ask how things were going with Chad's health.

"Well, I'm a little nervous, because today we'll likely find out if the cancer has come back. They should call this afternoon with the results." I couldn't look her in the eye in fear of bursting into worried tears over our Starbucks coffees.

She sighed compassionately. "Oh, Megan. Go home. Go home and spend the afternoon with him. You don't know what lies ahead of you. Make sure you take the time you need together while you know things are good. Don't just take the time when things are bad."

I was so appreciative of her tenderness towards me that I wanted in some weird way to thank her—so I continued to work for another half an hour before I couldn't stand replying to emails any longer.

It was like I had been holding my breath from the moment I woke up. When I walked through the apartment door, I let out a little air, relieving some of the pressure that had been building from not being with Chad.

On the patio, soaking up the sun, Chad was visiting with his friend. I looked at him when I came around the corner, searching his face. I could tell by the look he gave me that there was no news yet, and that this visit was a welcome distraction.

While Corey was in the bathroom, I asked for confirmation. "Have you heard anything yet?"

He was relieved and impatient at the same time. "No."

"You could call them, I suppose?"

I didn't know why I would suggest that. Hi, I was just calling to see if I have cancer?

"Yeah, I could; maybe if I don't hear from them by the end of day. I don't want them to call, but want them to. I'm scared, I guess."

245

Corey returned, and the topic changed.

Once he left, Chad slipped his smartphone into his hoodie pocket, and we headed out for a slow stroll along the river. We talked and talked about anything that came to mind—music, the river, how long some of the houses had been there —anything that wouldn't allow for a pause or silence in the conversation.

Riiing Riiiinnnggg Riiiiinnnnggggg.

He looked over at me as I took a deep breath. There was so much silence; I swear the river halted.

He let it ring a few times before picking up. "Hello?"

"This is he. Yes, okay. I see. Sure. Yeah, tomorrow works. Two o'clock? Yeah, that's fine. Okay. Thanks."

Click.

His eyes met mine

Even though the call display showed the caller was from the hospital, I still asked who it was.

"Oh, just the clinic. My platelets are low, so they wanted to book me in for a transfusion. It was just the receptionist. They don't have results for me."

Knowing the clinic would soon close and the results would have to wait, we went back to holding our breaths for another day.

I DON'T KNOW WHAT TO SAY.

My knees went weak as I set down my bag and looked at Chad sitting on the couch.

"I don't know what to say."

Oh, please no.

I could feel the blood surging through my heart. "They say my counts are coming back. It explains why I've been feeling so shitty these past few days."

The colossal disappointment hit me like a punch to the gut. I need to hear a plan. I need to hear that this is manageable and that we'll be back to our new life in no time.

"They're going to see if they can get me back on that trial drug, Revlimid, that I was on a few years ago."

"That one that gave you really bad neuropathy?" I remembered how increasingly tingly his feet had grown, leading to irreversible nerve damage and all the cramping.

"Yes, but they've made improvements on the side effects since I was last on it. Last time my counts were too high for it to work, but since I've had a transplant, I might be eligible." Even though his delivery of the plan was optimistic, his disappointment leaked through.

That night we went to bed after distracting ourselves with our nightly habit: whatever HBO show we were keeping up with, followed by TMZ. But once in bed, he in his spot on the right and I in my spot on the left, sleep was far away.

By the time morning rolled around and our alarms went off, it felt like we had been awake for hours. I rolled over, propped myself up on one elbow, and looked down at him.

"Do you want to get married?"

I didn't know what was happening here, but if we could do anything that would bring the summer light back into our life, I would do it.

He rested on his back, latched on to my hand, and looked in my eyes before looking down at our hands. "No," he said softly. "I wouldn't do that to you."

I didn't have a whole lot to say about that. I wasn't sad that he said no; I was sad that he wanted to protect me from something I never needed protecting from. I just wanted for us to be as welded together as possible.

We tried to resume our healthy routines of summer—walks, dinners, workouts—but everything we did had a haze over it as we returned to the test, wait, result cycle. The vibrancy of good health was now blurred, and we waited for a plan to get us out of idling and back on the road to recovery.

The sun started setting earlier and rising later. Chad did too. Naps were part of his routine again as his energy levels declined.

Fewer dinners out, more dinners in. It felt like we were preparing for hibernation.

CLAPPING SO HARD, BLINKING AWAY TEARS.

My friend Eva had been living with cystic fibrosis since we shared a ballet class when we were five. I didn't understand the disease, nor would it have made a difference if I had. She was awesome—no illness could hide that from anyone.

After college, with both of us back in Vancouver, we reunited in the bedroom of her family's house, sharing stories of mutual crushes and hospital war stories. But my time in the hospital as a caregiver paled in comparison to the time she had spent over the years as a patient.

Eva shared exciting updates about a documentary that was being made about her struggles with cystic fibrosis and waiting for and receiving a double lung transplant.

September 2009 didn't just bring heart-wrenching news for Chad. It also brought news for Eva. Nearly two years after receiving her transplant, a gift of life, her body was rejecting her new lungs.

When the Vancouver International Film Festival's debuted Eva's story, *65_RedRoses*, she generously gave Chad and I her last two tickets to the Friday night screening. Neither she nor Chad was in the good health they had been in just months earlier, but that night they were both in good spirits.

She greeted us with a vibrant smile that made her breathing tubes and the oxygen tank hooked to her wheelchair barely noticeable.

When the film was over, Chad let go of my hand and joined in the standing ovation. He was clapping so hard, blinking away tears, as Eva stood up out of her wheelchair and walked to the front of the theatre. It was one of the most moving moments I had ever experienced.

Chad was one of the last people standing, as if the longer and harder he clapped, the more admiration he could express.

Chad left the theatre that night a changed man. Seeing *65_ RedRoses* made him recognize that you could talk about a disease without being the disease. Eva had cystic fibrosis; it was not who she was. And when she shared her challenges, it wasn't an imposition. It was powerful.

I JUST FEEL LIKE I'VE
GOT CANCER.

"So, looks like I'm good to go for Revlimid. They'll see what my counts are doing in another month and decide if they can keep me on it. If it doesn't work, things start to get really scary."

Backup was on its way. There was also great encouragement that this drug could work: it had kept Chad's mom's multiple myeloma stable for years now.

Our only hope was that the cancer wasn't too big for the drug. We'd have three weeks before the first cycle was over, and then blood work would show what we hoped would be an outstanding response to the treatment.

When I asked Chad how he felt, he'd say, "It's hard to describe, but it's different than the flu or anything else. I just feel like I've got cancer."

Fortunately, one month later, the blood tests showed that Revlimid had slowed the growth of the cancer. His counts hadn't dropped, but they had stalled.

Hope had arrived. The (back-up) plan was working.

YOU'VE GOT TO BE KIDDING!

Chad's voice was lighthearted as he spoke to someone at the clinic about his blood work.

With the light from the window shining onto his pale skin, he looked at me and chuckled.

I smiled back. "What?"

"Ha…so my blood test just came back, and it shows that I've got fucking swine flu." He put his hand to his forehead and shook his head. "Jesus Christ."

I mirrored his headshake. "You've got to be kidding! How much crap can they find in your blood, eh?" I scooted closer to him. We were half-smiling, not because it was humorous, but because receiving news like this on top of everything else pushed us into un-fucking-believable territory.

Swine flu, more scientifically referred to as the H1N1 virus, had been making international headlines for its vicious effects. Flu viruses are always very hard on the immune-suppressed: old people and sick people. And Chad was no exception.

They put Chad on an antibiotic in addition to the rest of his cancer cocktail, but otherwise there was little to be done. We'd just have to wait it out.

If you've ever been sick for more than four days, you know how time loses relevance. Time between the couch, chair and bed. Time for one fizzy drink to wash down another round of pills. Time is measured in comfort, TV shows, and how long you can talk to someone without being exhausted. I knew this because I also got swine flu. Un-fucking-believable.

It slowed me down, fast and hard. For the first time in a long while, I saw life through a patient's eyes.

ME, MYSELF AND MYELOMA

Chad's Blog
October 30, 2009

I've decided to put it all out there, whether it reaches anyone or it's just a way for me to get it out so I find some peace.

I've been battling cancer and all that goes with it since I was 26, just a kid, two years out of university. I was in the typical post-university gloom, trying to adjust to the real world. I spent too much time in the weight room and in bars on the weekend, binge drinking and doing a poor job of picking up ladies.

After bouncing around several shitty odd jobs for the first year after university, I finally landed a so-called "career" job with a multinational company, working in an office with 50 of the most unhappy, unhealthy people you've ever seen.

That lasted eight months before I couldn't take it anymore and left to coach tennis, something I had done in the summers during high school and university. The money was good, the freedom was better, the sun and the people were fantastic. I had a love-hate relationship with tennis at the time, but that's another story.

I had settled down and was living with my girlfriend Katharine (who is a special person and is still a close friend). Things were going well, except for the horrendous debt I had accumulated in just a few short years. Student loans spent on beer and lame 90's clothes—a line of credit spent on a month-long trip back to the States, where I bought a car—a credit card maxed from eating out. Let's say $30,000. Then everything changed forever—just like that....

Here we go...I have nothing to hide.

D-Day was May 17, 2001. After months of testing for everything under the sun, I was diagnosed in the late stages of a cancer I'd never heard of, multiple myeloma. The crazy thing is that I had just lost a close friend two years earlier to testicular cancer. And now me!?

Jay was everyone's best friend and the most amazing guy—it makes me cry to think of him, but I'm glad he will never be forgotten. I was dating his sister Katharine when I first got sick.

It's strange to think back to that diagnosis. Hundreds of words were said by the doc, and all I remember is CANCER and my mother asking if it was TERMINAL. There is no cure for multiple myeloma, but there are treatments that can keep you going in hope they keep coming up with new ones. The average lifespan for mm patients is five years...so they say. I don't believe it's fair to give people timelines and percentage chances of surviving this and that. You can never underestimate the human will to live....

Megan's Blog

Chad has recently started writing his story on a blog. He is finally talking, telling and explaining what his life has been like while living with multiple myeloma for the past nine years. Thank goodness.

I see how therapeutic it is for him to be writing. I also see how many people care about him and care about what is going on in his life. Perhaps I should have started a long time ago, when the 'fairy tale' really started getting complicated, but for some unknown reason, I am just sitting down now. I'm going to be honest—and just write about the way it is.

I don't want to write this blog so people feel compelled to read it, or feel they need to understand it—but for those who are curious and never ask, for those who ask and I brush off, or perhaps for those who have been in my shoes and know what it's like— that's why I'm writing.

And when I write, it helps me sort out this mess in my head.

JUST FUCKING TORTURE

Chad's Blog
October 30, 2009

Megan and I have had a very rough 24 hours. We both have the swine flu, and it takes a lot to knock her down. I've never seen her totally out of commission before. But today she is watching episode after episode of Gossip Girl and recovering nicely.

I was taken into the hospital by ambulance yesterday with swine flu, congestive heart failure, pneumonia, poor kidney function…and the cancer problem, which has been escalating lately.

Once again, the doctors gave it to me straight, and for many hours yesterday I thought I'd never make it home again to be with Meg. After you run through the emotions, the fight begins, and there is no other option but to make it out of there.

I've been in these situations more times than I care to remember, and each time I've been lucky to come out of it. But it does take its toll on the mind and body, and I have felt myself deteriorate with each challenge.

Facing your mortality is life-changing. Facing it over and over is just fucking torture. In the past nine years I've had two bone marrow transplants, total body radiation and many rounds of chemo. I've been on and off steroids and had every myeloma treatment available. I'm running out of options. Ten months ago I had my second transplant from my original donor. I owe him the life he's given me.

Things went bad and I spent several weeks in intensive care, then several more in cardiac care. It was the craziest time, but Meggie hung in there with me and we got through it.

I can't even imagine the torture this has put her through. The months after proved to be even more trying for us since I required so much help. Meg was just starting a new job, and then she had to come home to this creature, curled up in a ball, who couldn't feed himself. She would stand behind me with calming words while I moaned and screamed while trying to pee out blood clots the size of slugs. She has endured night after night of cramping that brought me to tears from the pain while she rubbed me and brought me electrolyte drinks. It is a 24-hour job for both of us. I just want to give her the life she deserves; that's why I fight so hard now.

Can you imagine being her, dealing with this day in and day out? She's the most special person I've ever come across, and she's just getting started.

She's my confidant, my support, my love.

PANICKING

On Thursday, I thought Chad was going to die.

We had a few close calls during his second transplant in December, but this was the worst one yet. We were both home and sick with H1N1. For the first time in years, I was so sick that all I could do was lie on the couch. I wanted someone to pet me, bring me tea, and make my aching go away. Not really an option when the person who might otherwise be petting, fetching and loving is worse off than you are.

And when I say worse off, I don't mean he's coughing more than me or he's more tired than me, I mean his heart is erratic, he can't stand up without dipping in and out of awareness and he is starting to cry because he's getting weaker and weaker by the hour. (And when you see a tattooed, 34-year-old man who is usually an emotional rock start to cry because he's panicking, it's not a good thing.)

After attempting to get Chad comfortable lying on the floor (because sitting up was making him dizzy) we called his nurses and his doctors to try to figure out what to do. I could drive him to the clinic? Nope, he was too weak to make it to the elevator and down to the car. Should we just wait and see if he feels better in the next while, then take him in? Nope, Chad knows his body, and when he starts to panic, it's time to do something. We called 911.

I've had to make calls on Chad's behalf before. But the second the dispatcher asked what the problem was and the words, "my boyfriend is a blood cancer patient, and he has the swine flu," came out of my mouth, the reality of the situation set in and the tears started flowing.

With Chad in the background telling me what to say, I tearfully answered the dispatcher's questions. "Yes, he is conscious; yes, he is breathing; yes, he has tested positive for H1N1; yes, he is talking; no, he is not vomiting blood."

I hung up the phone and started gathering the things he would need: meds, hoodie, shoes, wallet. I've now choked back my tears and switched into operation mode. We can hear the sirens coming toward our apartment. Chad lightheartedly says, "Oh, here they come, they are coming for me." I look over at him, and as if he has just realized what he said, he has his hands on his head and tears coming down his cheeks. My heart cracks a little more each time I see him cry. He is such a strong person; when he cries, it's really bad.

The paramedics arrive, bringing the fire department with them.

Once the paramedics realize I'm also sick with H1N1, they throw on their masks. Our apartment feels like a scene from Grey's Anatomy with all the masked people around.

They run down the laundry list of questions with Chad, who is still on the floor, before lifting him onto a stretcher and carrying him into the elevator.

I decide to follow behind in my car. I walk back into the apartment to make sure I have everything, and the full scope of what has just happened hits me. The tears start again. I am by myself in an empty apartment, crying; I am sick, still coughing, and my boyfriend is en route to the emergency ward. This sucks.

At Lions Gate Hospital Emergency, I put on a mask, sanitized my hands, and went to look for Chad. Emergency is full of face-masked people, coughing and looking very sick. I hope they've got Chad in a room, because he can't be around this many sick people.

I walk down the hall, ignoring the nurse who is scolding me: "If you are sick, go home; you can't be here."

I find Chad lying on a stretcher in the hallway. No doctors, no nurses, no one—he's all alone.

What. The. Hell.

As I make sure he has his meds and wait to hear what the plans are, I think, *I wish you were at VGH. They know you, your doctor is there, they know what to do. They wouldn't leave you in the hall.* But Chad is generally very trusting of the people who take care of him, so he assures me that they have things under control here.

And he tells me to go home. I can't be there if I'm sick, he says, and I need to get myself a doctor. The paramedics come by and tell me the same thing. They say that they have a bed ready for him, but I can't go in.

Great. Just great.

I understand why I have to go home, but it still hurts to be shooed away when all I want is to be there to make sure he gets better.

We have a quick, tearful kiss on the cheek goodbye and they wheel him away. That was it. I walked to the entrance of emergency to wait for my mom.

I'm so tired and emotional at this point that I just pace in front of emergency, waiting for my mommy. (It's funny how 'Mom' turns into 'Mommy' when something is really wrong.) She comes, and I cry harder.

We walk around to have coffee and pick some food up for Chad before returning to the hospital. She goes in to see Chad while I sit in the waiting room with my mask on and my hoodie pulled over my ball cap.

Finally I went to say hi to Chad through the glass of his room while my swine-flu-free mom sat beside him. I read his lips through the glass: "Go home, you can't be here, go get better."

Feeling better that Chad is being taken care of, has food and is comfortable, I am looking forward to having a night on the couch. By tomorrow, all will be right with the world.

I put my pajamas on, put on the first episode of Gossip Girl, and talked to Chad on the phone. He's getting tests done, we'll be in touch. Good.

Less than an hour goes by and Chad calls again. He gets out "Hi, babes," and then silence. All I hear is him choking back tears. "I'm sorry, I just need a second."

Fuck.

"The doctors just came in to see me, and they are really, really worried about me. I have pneumonia in my lungs, and my kidneys are failing, and I'm in congestive heart failure again."

These were all the same problems he had last year after the transplant, so we are well aware of how sick this means he is.

"They are going to run some tests, but the doctor just said he was sorry. I don't know what's going to happen. I love you so much."

He is now sobbing uncontrollably. "I don't know, I don't know, I don't know. I just want to come home to you. You know how much I love you, right? You know when I get upset, it's not me talking, right? I just want to get better for you."

I am pacing around the apartment, repeating the same thing, "I love you, I'm going to come there, I love you, I'm going to get my things." But I know I can't, because they won't let me in. "Promise me that you are going to come home to me."

"I can't promise anything," he said. "But I know that if something happens, you are going to be okay."

I'm not okay. I'm not going to be okay. Oh. My. God. This is not what I thought was going to happen to my life. I am supposed to grow old with this person, travel the world with this person, marry and have babies with this person—and here I am saying goodbye *over a cell phone*!?!?!?

We are both sobbing.

Eventually, we calm each other down, saying that we'll talk the entire night. We'll just stay on the phone, and we won't be alone. I've sunk to the floor, on my knees, rocking back and forth. And when he hangs up so he can rest, I just lay there on the floor.

After calling my mom again, I pulled myself off the floor and impulsively went to our bedroom. I opened my jewelry box and put on every necklace and bracelet Chad had given me. I went back to the kitchen counter, flipped open my journal and wrote:

To my Chad:

To my groom, to my other half,

You, sir, are one of a kind.

You are one of the kindest, most generous people I have ever known and you make me feel like a princess.

You have handled the curve balls that life has thrown at you with strength, discipline, courage and determination. Yet you also tell stories that put people at complete ease and make them laugh so hard they cry, or leave them thinking, "Did he really just say that?"

I love you. I cannot tell you in words how proud you make me, how much I admire you, how often you are in my thoughts and how much your love has changed me forever.

To the man who owns my heart—I look forward to the next seven decades. To being your wife, listening to your stories, loving you and—of course—making fun of you.

I think this must be like when someone finds out a person they love has died in an accident. "I didn't plan for this, I didn't get to say what I needed to say." Understanding the severity of Chad's situation during his transplant, I had to process the fact that death was a possible outcome. But other than a few hours of fear, I never really thought it would happen. And I thought that, if it came to that, we would always have time to come to terms with it—together.

This was not how I imagined it.

On a cell phone?

Chad called again, saying he had spoken with a new young resident doctor who made him feel better and gave him a little hope that he'd get out of there.

When Mommy came to comfort me for the second time that day, Chad was feeling less scared, and I was too. We ate a little, drank a little and watched a movie. Chad told me that he was tired and was going to try to get some sleep, so I should try to do the same.

Sleep? Yeah, right. This is my biggest fear. I'm home. Chad's not. I don't know if he is ever coming home. I am glued to my phone, worried that if I fall asleep I'll miss *The Call*. What if the doctors call and tell me I need to come because he is dying? What if Chad calls me, scared. What if he dies in his sleep and we never get to say goodbye?

But eventually I cry myself to sleep, exhausted and worried. I haven't slept uninterrupted for the past week because Chad's heart has been acting funny, and he's been worried that he might have a heart attack in the middle of the night. Which means that I am worried he's going to have a heart attack in the middle of the night. If I haven't been up to help him with the cramping, I've still been waking up every few hours, just to make sure he's still breathing. I shift in bed to make sure he shifts, or put my arm across him just to make sure he moves.

I am exhausted. I sleep, but wake up every few hours to check my phone. At 5:30 in the morning, I text him to see if he's awake. I get a message around 8:00 a.m. saying he got some rest.

We made it through the night.

His kidneys have calmed down a little, he reports, and the doctors are going to send him home today.

I'd like to say that after the 24 hours we had, we collapsed into each other's arms, told each other how thankful we are and kissed passionately. I'd like to say that everything is better now.

But this is just the start of the week.

UNTIL WE MEET AGAIN...

Chad's Blog
October 31, 2009

I don't even know where to begin this. Being sick is such a selfish thing and I've had a hard time dealing with that. I have a lot of guilt because I've had to miss some of my best friends' weddings, the births of their children and other major events in their lives because I haven't been well enough. I'm so tired of that bullshit excuse, and I think at some point I began to withdraw from people because I didn't want to disappoint them anymore. At times I can look quite well to the outside world, but looks are deceiving.

There have been stages in the past nine years where I've had some treatments give me a better life, especially early on, but the past three or four years have been rocky. It's hard because, as time goes on, people have families and advance in their careers. All I can say is that I'm still fighting cancer, still waiting to start my life. Don't get me wrong—I worked up until a year ago and did what I could to advance myself. I was very grateful to have a forgiving workplace. But I didn't have the energy to fully commit because I needed to use that energy to fight.

Anyway, I'm really grateful to all my friends, from Lethbridge to West Van High, my North Van gals, my Louisiana life (my home away from home), the North Shore Winter Club and my Hollyburn peers. I've learned so much from you, and you've given me so much support. I really appreciate you all and the laughs we have shared…so many laughs. That's what I enjoy about Facebook—you can keep up with everyone from as far back as you remember, see their children, their wedding photos. Everything they're willing to share is available for viewing. I guess I just want people to know I'm thinking of them on their special days and that I often reflect on our times together…'cause I got time to think…'cause that's what I do! Just 'cause you don't hear from me doesn't mean I don't care and that I don't tell Megan all our crazy stories. Looking forward to new stories and more laughs. Until we meet again…

I HAVE NO TEARS LEFT.

Megan's Blog
November 4, 2009

Chad came home, but I was still sick and he was very weak. The past 24 hours had made him more emotional than I have ever seen him. Without exaggeration, everything upset him. Ev-er-y-thing.

He was so weak that I had to pull up to the door to drop him off; he couldn't walk the 50 yards from my parking space. We took slow steps to the elevator, slow steps to the apartment and slow steps to the couch. He was upset that he was weak, he was upset that the apartment wasn't clean. We were both sick with the same thing, so doing laundry and cleaning the door handles, as he wanted, seemed hopeless to me. But I wasn't about to say that, so I went at it: laundry and cleaning, swine-flu style.

So no, there wasn't a leap into each other's arms or an "I'm so happy you are alive" moment. It was a messed-up, Cinderella-y moment.

But once he saw that hauling laundry downstairs was making me wheeze and cough, his anger and frustrations melted. He just wanted a hug. "You're sick, too. I'm sorry, baby."

The afternoon slipped away. Chad was more comfortable, and I was more tired. I curled up on the couch and watched a serious amount of Gossip Girl while he wrote on his blog. He wrote and wrote and cried and cried. Writing about everything that has gone on, and is going on, brought many emotions to the surface. He was most upset when he clicked 'share'—Chad is such a private person, so making the decision to share his story with anyone was very emotional for him.

It's funny. After that terrible night and seeing Chad so upset at home, I've dried right up. I have no tears left. I don't know why. Maybe it's because I'm in fighting mode. Maybe it's because when he can't be strong, I have to be. Maybe it's both of those. I'm not sure.

But what I am most sure about is that after that awful Thursday night phone conversation, after thinking I was saying goodbye to Chad, some part of me died. I don't know how else to describe it.

Whether Chad and I live long and happy lives together or this all ends terribly, that feeling will haunt me. I don't know if I will ever forget it.

They took him off Revlimid because they said it was conflicting with the H1N1 medications and causing his heart to work improperly. Knowing how hard it was to get approved for the drug, I hated this. It may solve the current problem, but will likely be more of a problem down the road.

I suppose getting him through H1N1 was the priority. Cancer was second. Or maybe it was all the same fucking thing. This whole thing is just a poisonous storm.

LET'S WATCH HIM FRY.

Chad's Blog
November 1, 2009

My sister Jen and her husband, Bill, came to town with the kids this weekend for some Vancouver Halloween action. My niece Lauren is eight and my nephew Ben is six. I've been excited for them to come, as I don't see them much since they live in Edmonton.

I was disappointed that they'd come all this way and I wouldn't get to see them. But I rested up yesterday, picked up some fireworks, and Meg and I made our way over to the parentals where all were gathered for the evening festivities.

A block from my parents' home, a whole street of houses put on a Halloween party. It was very impressive, with hundreds of people milling about trick or treating. My niece and nephew thought it was the greatest, and maybe I did, too.

I then proceeded with my humble fireworks show, which turned into a huge laugh as everyone stood on the back deck with me just below, lighting these unpredictable mini-cannons off. The area we were in is very small and these things were going off at eye level to the family, who were in hysterics every time one went awry, sending us all scampering for cover.

My mother was laughing so hard she tried to go inside and walked straight into the closed sliding glass door head first—and kept laughing hysterically…she is the greatest.

Unfortunately, things turned quickly. As soon as Meg and I got in the car to leave, my heart began to beat out of control. I was still breathing okay, but it was jumping out of my chest, making me very uncomfortable. We made it home, and I lay on the bed with the heart rate monitor on, trying to relax. My heart rate fluctuated between 145 and 200 beats per minute, and it wasn't settling.

We called 911 and off I went for the second time in three days, bouncing around in the back of the ambulance, answering the same fucking questions I've been answering for years. They got me in quick, for which I'm grateful, but for two hours my heart rate jumped around, sometimes over 200 beats per minute, never below 150. I couldn't lie down because fluid in my body had been building, surrounding my heart and lungs so I couldn't breathe. I sat on the edge of the gurney with my legs dangling, trying to find comfort…it was so exhausting. I could hear the nurses and doctors discussing what to do while I guided them on my history as best I could. They seemed eager to shock my heart into a better rhythm, but I didn't think it was safe, so they tried various meds to slow things down.

Finally, after four hours, the meds began to settle things enough that I was more comfortable. I was so thirsty and they couldn't give me any fluids until things calmed down in case they had to use the shock pads. Really, I think they just wanted to try those things out, because that's all they kept talking about. Let's watch him fry 'cause I'm bored—I suppose if I worked there, then that would be entertaining. They did a good job, and they finally brought me the best apple juice I've ever had. And I could finally lie down.

They let me go this morning, although my heart rate is still high, at 120. Tomorrow I will be in touch with my doctor, who will set up my new plan of action.

Again, I'm just happy to be home and around Megan. My situation is putting so much stress on her, as my main caregiver, so I will find a way to make it easier. She does so much for me, and I'm putting her through hell. I'm glad she is out enjoying the sunshine.

HERE WE GO AGAIN.

I was on the mend, and Chad was home. All the chaos of the last two days felt like it was settling down. His family was in town from Edmonton to "Go twick-or-tweeting with Unctle Chad," according to Ben.

In true fighter fashion, Chad rested for all of Halloween day to muster up enough energy to light off fireworks for his niece and nephew. And boy, did he deliver.

As though he was in perfect health and had the same amount of energy as his six-year-old nephew, Chad lit off a whole bunch of fireworks as the rest of us watched from his parents' deck.

Thanks to the erratic bursts of flames from the inexpensive fireworks, I saw Chad laugh harder and move quicker than I had since the summer evening we walk-raced to his parents' house. It was fun to see that—under all that man, there was still a little boy.

Feeling good about being able to put on a show for the kid-dos, we left his parents' house with promises of "See you in the morning!"

We hadn't driven more than a block when I saw Chad start feeling his chest.

Uh oh.

He said, "It's okay, just feels a little quick. I may have overdone it."

We got into the apartment, and he went straight to the bed to lie down.

He lay there, still feeling his chest. I grabbed my running heart-rate monitor to see how fast his heart was beating, because when I put my ear to his chest, it sounded like some new dub step beat. We put the monitor on, and within seconds it started flashing 190. (I couldn't help but feel a moment of envy when it also reported Chad had just burned four calories in four seconds.)

We called the ambulance. Here we go again.

"Yes, he's breathing; yes, he's talking; no, he's not vomiting blood." In the same way I gather my things to go to the gym, or get ready for work, I gathered his meds, his hoodie, and his shoes. Strange how quickly things become 'normal.' This time, I'm not crying.

When I hear the paramedics at our door, I open the door and let out a gasp. Standing there are two women with knives in the heads, their hair covered by bloody bandages. With their uniforms and a stretcher.

Happy Halloween, you crazies.

They come in, run Chad's vitals and loudly joke with one another as they stomp their dirty boots on our cream carpet. They shave a bunch of hair off Chad's arm to put the IV in and leave the hair on the bed.

There I was again. Empty (messy) apartment. By myself. Boyfriend on his way to the hospital. Still sick.

Knowing how much Chad had wanted a clean place to come home to two days ago, I vacuumed the floor and bed before picking up our coats and heading for Lions Gate Emergency again.

Shouldn't I be dressed in some petite animal costume skipping down Granville Street tonight?

IT'S BEEN SKETCHY AT HOME.

Chad's Blog
November 3, 2009

Today I was admitted to cardiac care at VGH. Things aren't mending on their own, so action is being taken. Three teams of doctors are now following me, including cardiologists, kidney specialists and my BMT doctors. I'm grateful to our health system and the care I continue to receive. My headspace is clear and I'm comfortable, except for my ass from being on it the past week.

Of course, there are a million places I'd rather be than in another hospital bed, but I know what I need to do in order for that to happen. I'm not bitter, not sad—just bound and determined to live out my dreams. Meg came by tonight with my things, some snacks and the computer so we got to hang out and relax. She looks more at ease—I think she's relieved that I'm here, with people are monitoring me. It's been sketchy at home with my health so erratic. She's been taking care of me non-stop, and vigilant at watching me through the night. It has to be exhausting. I'm tired now and have much writing to do tomorrow......................good night

IT'S NOT SEXY AND IT'S NOT FUN.

I picked Chad up after a second night spent in emergency. He felt pretty good, but was naturally still worried about his heart, which had stabilized to about 120 rather than the remixed 190.

He said that the doctors and nurses really wanted to give him 'the paddles' to try and reset his heart rate into a regular beat. He had to talk them off that cliff.

I really worry in situations like that. If he were unconscious or unable to explain what was going on with his body after years of cancer treatment, it's possible some seriously bad decisions could be made.

We spent two days at home. On the second night, being the lovely man he is, he waited until he was really uncomfortable and scared before waking me up, even though he'd been awake and panicking for about three hours before.

We decided not to call the ambulance and to just wait it out until his appointment that morning with his cancer doc.

They decided the best thing was to admit Chad to VGH so they can keep a close eye on him. He spent two nights in cardiac care and is now up in the bone marrow transplant ward. It's a much better place, with nurses who know him and a room with a TV and a gorgeous view of the city.

He's still H1N1 positive, so everyone has to "suit up" before going in and out of his room. It's not sexy, and it's not fun. That being said, he's got some super-trooper friends who visit him anyway. Face masks or not, they are there for him.

It's weird seeing him, because he is stable now, but if they don't get the fluid away from his heart and kidneys and his cancer under control soon, he's in trouble. Big trouble.

I've been visiting him at night, but I feel like he's only half there. It's like half his brain is always focused on the fight. We talk, but it's either about what I did that day or what the doctors have said to him about his test results. We tried to watch a movie.

Although it was short-lived, resting my head on his shoulder, holding his hand, and laying on that stupid, single bed was the best both of us have felt in the last few days.

COMING BACK TO LIFE

Chad's Blog
November 4, 2009

I'm not the only one in my family to have been dealt the cancer blow. Within one year of my diagnosis, both my parents faced their own challenges. My father was hit quick with emergency surgery to remove a tumorous kidney—he was lucky it was caught before spreading to the other kidney. Four weeks later, he was hiking on a local mountain. He never speaks of it, but the memory of seeing him in so much pain has never left me. He has been a rock for all of us, and I can't imagine how hard it's been for him to provide care for both my mother and me—and to remain sane. He's retired now and living well—he's missing a kidney, but he's never been stronger.

A few months after my dad, my mother was diagnosed with multiple myeloma. She had been unwell for a number of years, so in some strange way I felt relieved that we had some answers. Myeloma can smolder in people for many years before becoming active, and I'm sure this was the case for my mom and maybe even me.

My mother's fight with the disease is the most inspiring I've ever heard of for a myeloma patient. She was 60 and had a bone marrow transplant from herself, where they took out some of her marrow, cleaned it up and put it back in. Things started off okay, but soon she got sick, then really sick with a nasty lung infection. Her treatment for the lung infection alone went on for a year. By Christmas of that year, 2002, she weighed less than 100 pounds and had endured a mild heart attack. She was days away from leaving us, and we were preparing for the worst.

I remember my sister and I begging her to start eating more, and she just couldn't. Slowly, with Dad tending to her every need with his amazing strength and patience, she began coming back to life. Over the course of the next few years, she just kept getting stronger, and to this day I swear she's still improving. She looks fantastic and has been taking a myeloma drug that has given her life back and has taken the cancer down to a point that it's barely detectable. She plays bridge, gardens and cooks for the family when everyone comes to town.

I couldn't put into words how big a comeback this was. I never realized how strong and competitive my mother is, but I know now…and I bow to the master!

So much happened between my first and second transplant. I had some healthier years as I recovered after the first transplant, but it wasn't long before the cat came back in summer of '04. I began a barrage of treatments, everything available for multiple myeloma. Some worked for a while, but sooner or later it would be time to try something else.

My quality of life fluctuated depending on the treatment and its side effects. I was in and out of the hospital. Sometimes daily visits were the norm. Other times it might be once a month. I've had hundreds of blood transfusions over the years to keep me going.

I encourage everyone to donate blood regularly as so many people out there are dependent upon it.

I've been on and off steroids, sometimes ballooning up like I'd been eating fast food for a month. This disease has been a part of my everyday life for almost nine years and I've had to embrace it. I've always considered it my job, except I don't get paid.

Despite it, I've done my best to maintain a normal life, working and staying in the best shape I could at whatever stage I'm at. I've rehabbed my body countless times and have always measured my health by the quality of my workouts. I watch my diet, although it's tough at times because of nausea, steroids and drugs in general. Sometimes just eating is a good thing.

What's normal, anyway? I suppose for me it's going out for beers with friends, playing tennis, traveling, working and enjoying life. I've managed to do these things whenever possible and can't wait to continue with it. I've made my way back down south to visit friends, been to Mexico several times and went to New York for the 2008 U.S. Open. My biggest travel accomplishment to date was making it to Europe six months after my last transplant, but I'll get to that later.

In the summer of 2006, I was off treatment for a few months, so my buddy JJ and I played the men's Open Summer Tennis Circuit. It felt so good to compete and we managed to do okay, reaching a few finals and finishing as the number-three doubles team in B.C. for that year. I've enjoyed my nights out playing poker with friends and nights in watching our favorite HBO shows. I have a good life and would never take it for granted. I just don't want it to end!

SO HERE I AM.

2009 has proved to be the ultimate test. I started the year completely spent, with no ability to deal with anything. If it weren't for my enormous support network—nurses and doctors, my family, Megan's family, our friends and especially Megan—I wouldn't have made it this far. Over the years, I've gotten to know almost all of the BMT nurses and doctors. They've been there for me time and time again. They've kept me in line, laughed with me, hugged me, picked me up and carried me at my weakest moments...not sure I could ever thank them all properly, but I try.

Meg's parents have also played a crucial role over the past year. They had already been through enough before I came into the picture. I carry so much guilt that I've brought their daughter into this mess, but they continue to accept me and treat me like their own. I really enjoy spending time with them. Meg's mom, Brenda, always makes fantastic dinners, then sends us home with a bag full of groceries...she's the sweetest.

Her dad, Tony, has become a good friend and confidant to me and always has a positive take on the day. Her younger brother Bryn reminds me of myself at the same age and makes me laugh whenever I see him. He's always up to something, and I find myself living through him. He had some serious health issues not so long ago and has made a tremendous comeback. He's become a fantastic skier and is living the 22-year-old dream...what a guy.

Throughout the winter and spring, I worked hard on rehabbing my body by using strength bands and doing yoga and lots of walking. Megan or my dad would take me walking whenever I asked, and by May I was pumping it up some good-sized hills.

My goal was to be able to make it to Europe for Megan's cousin's wedding in early June. I was really feeling the pressure, as I knew it was a critical point in our relationship. If I didn't make that trip, Megan would have been devastated, and rightly so. I managed to keep it together, and got the okay from the docs. We had the most amazing trip—London, Paris and Amsterdam in 10 days, as that's all the time they could safely give me. I started to fade in the last two days of the trip and rested in the hotel, but it gave Meg some time to shop in Paris, so it all worked out.

I got home and became ill, spending the next few weeks on the couch. It was worth it. The rest of the summer was great—we enjoyed plenty of sunshine, several trips to the Okanagan and lots of time with friends.

But come September, I could feel something change, and soon my doctor gave me the news that I had relapsed. I can't say I'm not devastated. They started me on a drug that I tried before, but only for a short time. It was just a trial drug then, and I was quickly taken off due to low blood counts. It has since become a successful treatment for many myeloma patients, including my mother, but last week I had to stop because of swine flu complications. So here

I sit in the BMT ward, in isolation…still got the swine, waiting for the next plan of action to take care of this relentless myeloma. I'm feeling strong and ready for whatever they throw at me…I'm waiting!

MY INSPIRATION

Chad's Blog
November 6, 2009

Though I just started this blog, it's been in development for many years. I tried keeping a journal in the past, but my thoughts weren't coming out the way I wanted. So what changed...why now? I suppose it started with my desire to give back. So much has been done for me over the years, hundreds of thousands of tax dollars spent on my treatments; the time and energy of family, friends, nurses and doctors who continue to care for and support me.

As much as I appreciate everything, it has taken its toll on me. What is my purpose? To drain the system and everyone around me!? I'm still alive for a reason, and I've spent countless hours thinking about how I can make a difference. Slowly I realized that it wasn't going to happen overnight, it was going to happen little by little. I want to be there for people, help people...support people. Last year I promised myself I'd never say no to anything, and I'd do my best to be there for my friends no matter how I felt, within reason. I was so excited this past summer that I was able to make it to the wedding of my best friend from university.

Brennan lives in Texas. He stands 6'4" tall, weighs 265 pounds and looks like a defensive back in the NFL—probably could have been. His heart is as big as he is, and when I first got sick all those years ago, he came to see me three times in a six-month period. He would force food into me, as I was half the size I was in college and struggling to put weight back on. One visit I gained eight pounds thanks to him. Anyway, he met a beautiful girl, Amanda, who shares his interests and keeps him in check. I was still feeling pretty rough from the Europe trip, but I sucked it up and Meg and I flew down to share the experience with them and their families. I'm very close with his family and was so happy that Meg got to meet them all. It was a beautiful wedding and we had a blast.

Last year I began working with the VGH foundation to put together a plan to raise $1 million for multiple myeloma research. They have been fantastic in helping me develop a package that discusses my family, our struggle with this disease and why funding is needed if a cure is to be found. I'm very determined to reach this goal and know it's possible. I've met many patients over the years, each of whom has a story. It's for them that I've set out on this mission. Anytime I feel down, I think of all the faces of those I've met who are worse off than me.

Eva Markvoort: A few weeks back I had the privilege of attending the local premiere of *65_RedRoses,* a documentary about a beautiful young woman who's been battling cystic fibrosis all her life. If you know anything about this disease, you know how horrendous it is. Just a few years back, she had a double lung transplant in the hope of giving her a better life. Her spirit and the way she embraces life has impacted me greatly. I can only say: you need to watch this documentary.

Megan went to high school with Eva, and I was able to meet her that night. I wanted to say something to her, but nothing came out. I know what she's feeling and maybe nothing can be said—just a hug would suffice. She is now looking to have a second transplant, as her body has rejected the first. If anyone can make it through this, it's Eva. I think about her often and can't thank her enough for the strength she's given me.

James Mouat Sedgwick (Jay): It's been 10 years since Jay left us; he was only 24 years young when he passed. He fought a truly courageous battle with cancer, and I consider it a privilege to have been there to witness it. His strength continues to push me, and no matter how bad things get, my fight pales in comparison to his.

He went through more horrors in a three-month period than any human should experience in two lifetimes. His aorta blew twice—they cracked him wide open, and he came back both times. He was in a coma for weeks, and he came back again. The day before he passed was his birthday, and his family and close friends gathered in his room for a party.

For the first time in weeks, maybe longer, he was sitting up in bed, smiling and talking with us while palming a football in one hand. We all thought he'd made it—he had survived three months of the most horrific shit the human body could take. It was a day that none of us will forget. The next day I went to see him, and he looked tired as his mother rubbed his feet. I gave him a kiss on the cheek and told him I'd be back later to watch a movie. That was the last time I saw him. A few hours later his aorta blew for a third time, and after a scene I couldn't imagine, he was gone. If I accomplish anything in this life, it's because he is with me, driving me to be a better person—he's my inspiration!

A LOT OF TIME ALONE

Last night I picked up groceries and dinner for Chad after I left work. I was excited to see him. It's the same feeling as coming home to him after work—it's just that 'home' is a little different right now.

I arrived at his new room and followed the protocol: Gown. Mask. Gloves. Enter. There was the initial excitement of, "Hi baby - thanks for all the goodies," but he was in the mood to blog.

That's fine. I'll give you some time.

I went downstairs to pick up some muffins that friends had dropped off. Came back upstairs. Gown. Mask. Gloves. Enter. Still blogging.

Laura arrived with magazines for both of us, so I went and chatted with her for a while. Thank you, Matt and Laura.

Then, back to the room. Gown. Mask. Gloves. Enter. Still blogging.

Not wanting to interrupt or be confrontational by suggesting that he could blog later when he didn't have someone to hang out with, I just sat on the bed and read my new magazines.

He occasionally encouraged me to "go if you'd like." But I wanted to keep him company for as long as I could. He spends a lot of time alone in that room, so I figured he'd want company. But after an hour of minimal talking, I left with a kiss on his cheek.

"I'll text you later, baby," he said. "Thank you."

Gown off. Mask off. Gloves off. Put his goodies in the fridge. Leave. Pay 15 dollars for parking. Go to video store for therapeutic Gossip Girl fix. Video store closed. Whimper. Home. Couch. Alone. Oprah re-run. Sleep.

This sucks.

I understand that I'm not the priority. Nor should I be. Being alive is the only thing that matters. But I still can't help but feel sad. Sad for him, that he is fighting so hard; sad for our relationship, because when the going gets tough, it's the first thing to take a back seat; and sad for me, because I miss him. I miss the carefree summer we just had. I miss feeling sexy. I miss kissing, and our intimacy.

THE THINGS THAT

MOTIVATE ME

Chad's Blog
November 7, 2009

I'm trapped in this body that used to be capable of so much and could take me anywhere. I'm still an adventurous, competitive person underneath—one who thrives on physical activity and constant stimulation.

That may be the hardest thing I've had to let go of over the years. I want so bad to be able to step out on a court and play hard without worrying about the consequences to my body.

I want to make it to Australia come March to see my friends and explore that country. I want to work again and feel the satisfaction of accomplishing something each day.

I want to be able to keep up with Megan. I want to reach this fundraising goal and celebrate the victory. I want to see my niece and nephew grow up and maybe even have kids of my own. These are some of the things that motivate me to keep fighting. And this guy who keeps doing laps around the ward every hour—I'm coming for him as soon as they let me leave my room, and there's going to be some rubbing, "cause rubbing is racing."

I sit in this hospital room with only my thoughts. I'm tired of TV, sick of lying down and I've had enough chillin'. All I want to do is get out for some fresh air. Whenever I'd get sick as a kid, my dad would always tell me to go out and get some fresh air. There is definitely some short-term relief in that, but it may not solve all my problems. Today, though, I'd settle for some of that short-term relief and the rain on my face.

WATCHING. WAITING. WONDERING.

I'm sitting here in the hospital room with my ET suit on, watching Chad sleep, wishing he would magically pop up out of his sickly sleep and say, "All better now!"

I had a really good weekend. I spent time with friends and had a much-needed bar-star night with Adrienne on Friday: little dresses and lots of cocktails. Last night I had a cozy sleepover at Mom and Dad's. I also just took some time for myself. I don't really like being by myself most of the time, but the last few days I've enjoyed the silence and the time to think.

How can I make Chad happier? How much longer until he gets better? How much longer until 'we' get better? In the meantime, how do I make me better?

I've mentioned before how quickly some of this stuff becomes 'normal.' Chad is on a type of dialysis-plasma transfer thing right now, filtering out his blood and the cancer proteins, which they have recently found in his kidneys. In order to do this, they have put a dialysis cord in his neck. It's pretty creepy looking, but it almost looks normal now. He's lost so much weight and muscle that he's looking like he did around transplant time. That, too, starts looking normal. Similar to putting on shoes before leaving home, putting on a gown, gloves and mask has become normal. Visits to the hospital. Park. Elevator. Room. Sit. Chat a little. Drive. Home. Alone.

Normal.

The one thing that I cannot get used to, and that I certainly don't want to become normal, is 'sick Chad.' 'Sick Chad' is not the easygoing, self-sufficient, snuggly, can't-wait-to-hug-me guy I love. He's frustrated, unhappy and helpless, and he's going crazy being in that room all day long. Unfortunately, he can't help venting those frustrations onto me.

I can't get used to him saying things to me out of frustration, or not bothering to talk to me. That isn't 'my Chad,' it's 'sick Chad.' This might be the hardest thing of all. The only way I can think of describing it is that it's like being with someone who is drunk all the time while you are always sober. Things are said that he doesn't remember; I remember everything. I have learned to be very patient, but some days I worry my patience is running out.

Yet just when I start to think, "I can't take this anymore," 'sick Chad' disappears and 'my Chad' comes back to me, like the comeback king he is.

TO THE FOLLOWERS OF
THIS BLOG

Chad's Blog
November 9, 2009

Thank you for caring and for sharing your thoughts and words of support with Meg and I. I never thought anyone would be interested in this, and that was never the point, but it has turned out to be a very positive outlet for me. Most importantly, I've heard from so many people I haven't spoken to in years. I have so many memories with each of you.

Everyone faces adversity, everyone has a story—I just chose to share mine.

I want to say a special thank you to everyone involved with the fundraiser that's being held a few weeks from now at the Mosquito Creek Grill in North Vancouver. A young lady named Danielle Jenvey put this together—all I can say is that her mother Sharon raised a special lady. The money raised will be going towards my campaign to raise $1 million for multiple myeloma research. I also want to thank all our friends who continually show us support, bring cookies and muffins, books and DVDs. We are stocked for the year now.

I've been isolated in this room for a week, and I'm truly praying that the docs come up with something. I don't want this blog to be about my final days. I want to be writing about better days a few months from now. I'm a positive person and hate that I have no good news to report.

Bureaucracy is creeping into the process, which seems to happen more and more frequently. My doctor fights tooth and nail with hospital bigwigs for approval for me to receive certain treatments. It's scary to think my life is coming down to this.

I go through waves of panic, but then I become really competitive. I refuse to accept people telling me how sick I am—as long as they don't give up on me, I can make it. That's it: I'm scared to death they will give up on me. Too much money has been spent on me, too much time and energy. Bullshit. Keep me alive and I'll make a difference. The longer I'm alive, the more hope I can give other myeloma patients, the more awareness I can raise. Thanks for not giving up on me.

THE THREESOME

"It's as though you are in a threesome—a polygamist threesome," said one of my friends.

She was right. There are three of us in this relationship: Chad, me and myeloma.

I have to love whatever he comes with. I entered this relationship almost five years ago knowing very well that Chad already had a pre-existing lifetime partnership with myeloma. I know what I signed up for.

As our years together went on and his health improved, I became the number one wife in the relationship. Once in awhile, myeloma would come back, and I'd have to share him with her again.

Sometimes she would take priority, and I'd be left waiting for him to come back. Since his transplant and recovery, I have been the favorite. We had a brilliant summer together and a totally exclusive relationship. I was sooo happy.

Then September came around, and she came back. The threesome was on. We embraced it for a few months, him, her, me— trying to find a balance. But I'm afraid that, in the last week, she is full priority.

She is far more powerful than me, and I understand why he makes her such a priority. He has to. I wouldn't have it any other way, but that doesn't mean it doesn't hurt. It hurts knowing that he doesn't have energy to spend with me because he is so busy working on his relationship with her.

Yesterday was the first day in what has felt like months—even though it was really only a week—that Chad and I spent the day together, and myeloma took the back seat.

We laughed. He rubbed my back when I sat next to him. He held my hand. We kissed again. I left the hospital feeling so happy. I know he loves me. I know that she will leave again, and we'll be together soon.

BITTER SWEET

Chad's Blog
November 10, 2009

After another long day and many visits from the various doctors who are following my case, it was decided I could go home.
I was so happy to take in the fresh air as my dad pulled the car
around to the front of the hospital. For that moment I forgot about
everything, took in a few deep breaths and took a short walk to the
car—best I've felt in weeks.

Even the car ride home was fun. I felt like a little kid seeing
the city for the first time. I arrived home to a clean apartment
and Meg looking for a kiss. Our new couch arrived last week, so
I hadn't seen it yet and was so excited that it fit. It makes things
much cozier in this little apartment.

My friend Jesse and his wife Nicole arrived from Louisiana
today and came by for a visit tonight. It was so good to hang with
them. They're here all week, staying with family, so we should see
lots of them.

It's nice to be home, but I'm not feeling great; my kidneys
aren't improving and my disease is running wild. They still don't

have a plan for me, although my doc is working hard to find something. The cancer agency rejected a bid for a therapy that has helped me in the past, and now he's trying to get in touch with the company that makes it to see if they'll release some to me.

My cancer is very aggressive and every day counts, so I'm feeling like someone is kicking me in the stomach over and over—could also be constipation, but either way....

Anyway, I will take it hour by hour, day by day, and enjoy my time away from prison. Meg has the day off tomorrow and I'm expecting some visitors in the afternoon, so I'm excited for that. If I weren't so uncomfortable, things would be easier. But cancer has no conscience and feels no remorse for what it does to its victims. It's taking all my focus to keep it together, and all I really look forward to are those moments when I feel the symptoms ease and I can be myself.

HOME

My full-of-attitude, feisty boyfriend came home yesterday.

Although I was excited, I found myself nervously pacing the aisles at Whole Foods.

Do I have all the food that he likes? What are his cravings today? Do I have enough? What if I forget something and it was the only thing he wanted to eat?

I usually enjoy leisurely strolling through the store, sampling and buying things I don't need but am convinced will make me healthier and better looking, but this time I was far more anxious than any calming tea sample could soothe.

I know better than to think that when he comes home we will have a romantic "I'm so glad you're home!" moment. The best I can do is make our home clean and comfortable.

I thought that when Chad came home, I might relax and sleep better. *Wrong*. His belly is so distended, and they still don't know the cause. He can't lie down because fluid builds in his lungs and heart, so he can't breathe properly, and we had another largely sleepless night.

He is most comfortable upright on the couch, so I slept on the other couch beside him. I fell in and out of sleep, keeping one ear open for any lack of breathing. As the sun was rising, I looked over and found him on the couch in a deep, open-mouthed-fish sleep. After seeing that, I finally slept, too.

He seems a little more comfortable now. I'm watching him bop his head to songs on the radio that he describes as, 'songs I used to dance to in junior high while holding girls' asses.' Cute.

Then he looks over at me and says, "This one's for you:

"She drives me crazy - oooh oooh - but I just can't help myseeeeelllf!"

WHAT DID YOU JUST SAY?

I wanted to throw every pill bottle, pen and utensil on the counter at his face. I love him, but in that moment I hated him.

"What did you just say?" I tried to control my breathing.

"I said, it's like you're doing all this for the attention."

"Fuck you, Chad. You're an asshole." At that moment I meant every word, and as harshly and spitefully as I delivered them.

Tears in my eyes, I said, "Is that seriously what you think, Chad? You think I help pass you your meds, make sure you have food, get you water, sleep on the couch beside you so you're not scared—for the attention? Fuck you." Tears streamed down my cheeks.

"Ah, fuck, Meg, I'm sorry. Shit. Don't be mad." It was as though he'd been possessed by someone else for the last minute; he instantly knew what he said was wrong.

"I gotta go." I picked up my purse from the floor and left for work.

Adrienne got the first call. I was so pissed and hurt, and the poor girl had to hear all of it.

She reminded me of what I already knew. "You know he doesn't mean it. It's the drugs and the lack of sleep."

The complicated thing about words is that once you say them—no matter how much you would like to edit or delete what has been said—they'll never be unheard.

When I came home at lunchtime, he was sorry. Very sorry.

"You know, things are really tough right now. Maybe it would be best if you went back to your parents for awhile?"

Move out?

"It's just that this is a huge stress on us, and I understand it's a lot to handle."

"Who will take care of you if I leave?"

"I'll be ok. My dad can drive me and bring me food," he said unsurely.

"Then why don't you move to your parents' house? Why would I have to leave? I live here, and you're stuck with me, or I'm stuck with you."

He was trying not to smile.

And now we're back on the same page.

He lowered his head, "You're right, honey."

"We're in this together, Chaddy. I'm not leaving, so shut up about it already. This is tough, but we're going to get through it together, okay?"

In that moment, we fell in love again. After weeks of fighting the same battle, separately—we were back together. Our team was reunited, and we would fight to the death.

STRUGGLING...

Chad's Blog
November 12, 2009

I'm having a hard time getting comfortable. I hope that they'll give me something to take the edge off tomorrow—something powerful. Still no word on treatment, and things aren't getting better. It's an unexplainable feeling, being destroyed from the inside out. Each day I become weaker, but I never give up hope. I'm just wondering when something is going to happen. With every little ache or pain, I assume the worst. Getting up to go to the bathroom or kitchen is my workout; once I'm up, it feels good to stand. I think if I can get on some pain relief it will put me at ease. It's draining never getting a break, not being able to sleep. I've been sleeping out on the couch because it's the only way I can stay propped up, which is the most comfortable position for me right now.

Meg has been coming out to sleep on the other couch just to help comfort me...what do I say about that? We are doing our best and seem to have a good system going right now.

I'm overwhelmed by the messages I've been receiving, so know that I read them all with a smile. Right now it's game time, and all my energy goes to this.

LUCKY

Chad's Blog
November 13, 2009

I realize I can only control so much in my life. I control how I approach each day and the situations that arise, how I treat people and what I put into my body. Life can become pretty simple when it seems most complicated. There isn't time to think about the negative, no time to be angry; just time to appreciate everything and everyone around me. I can't say enough about how happy it has made me to read the words of so many people I love and respect.

Today I was desperate to get some relief, could no longer think straight...I needed help.

I had my scheduled appointment at the BMT day care unit, renamed the Krall Centre after Diana Krall's mother, who passed of multiple myeloma several years ago. Diana and her family have been a huge support, putting on extravagant events to raise money for the center. I've been lucky enough to meet her and her family—fantastic people. Anyway, my friend Katharine came over this morning to help me out while Meg was working...cause I'm a useless tit.

She was great—I wasn't up to talking much, but she got me food and helped me get ready for the clinic. I'd been anticipating this appointment for days, as I've become more and more uncomfortable. My dad picked me up and stayed with me to help sort things out. I was lucky today to get two of my favorite nurses. It makes such a difference. I've known them a long time and respect them immensely. They listened to me whine about everything and, soon enough, the doctors came in. Right away they put me on a med to drain fluid from my body; fluid buildup causes serious discomfort to a person with cardiac problems. They wrote me a prescription for hydromorphone, which takes the edge off and masks the real issues; fine with me. They set me up with appointments to see everyone following my case. What more can I ask?

My lead doctor came by for a visit and is working hard to find something for me. He's hoping for something early next week, knowing I can't wait much longer. My dad asked lots of questions, and I was grateful to have him there. We know they're doing their best, but we have to keep pushing them, too. I will go back in on Sunday for blood and platelet transfusions, and on Monday I will see the various specialists. As long as something is happening, I have a chance.

IT'S THE LITTLE THINGS
THAT MATTER.

With no answers and yet more waiting for possible treatment plans, life feels like it's on hold. It's a feeling that is all too familiar.

With all the uncertainties and frustrations of the past week, I've held onto sanity by realizing that 'big answers' and 'big solutions' are not going to come. They may come eventually, but they are not coming quickly. I have taught myself to be okay with this.

Thoughts of "what if?" and "what now?" can consume me, so I try to focus on the little things to keep me happy and sane. But the little things can also be frustrating.

Little things like when he's too uncomfortable and doesn't want to hug me, or is too nauseated to kiss me. Some days he is short-tempered and doesn't want to talk. At other times he wonders why I'm not talking to him.

Chad didn't choose this disease. He doesn't choose how much energy he has. He doesn't choose to feel this bad.

So while our situation tests my patience, it also gives me a great appreciation for the little things he occasionally has energy for. Like when he's too tired to talk, but strokes my hair when I sit beside him. When he thanks me, even if I haven't done anything. When he makes the effort to go to dinner, even if he has no appetite. Or when he mutters sleepily from the bedroom, "You look pretty," as I head out to work. These little things make me so happy. They are traces of a relationship that sometimes otherwise feels nonexistent.

I am anxious for the day when these little things happen all the time. Maybe if we are lucky we can start talking about the big things, too. But in the meantime, it's the little things that matter.

ONE LONG DAY

Chad's Blog
November 15, 2009

The past few weeks have become one long, continuous day. I take it hour by hour, constantly shifting, looking for the longest stretch of relief I can get out of one position. Sometimes I sit up, sometimes even stand, but mostly I lay propped up on my back. I enjoy it when I'm well enough to walk to the car for an appointment. It's more like a swagger, because I feel like a pimp in my baggy sweat pants and hoodie.

It never lasts. It quickly turns into a panicked shuffle as I become short of breath, desperate to sit down. The pain meds are masking reality and giving me some comfort. I've been nonexistent to Megan, just a drone who mutters occasional nonsense. Bedtime means nothing, just a continuation of the day as I slip in and out of a medicated state. I'm up every hour to pee, pace or move into a new resting position. Sometimes I turn on the radio, read or listen to the TV. The background noise dictates some entertaining dreamlike scenarios for me, which I enjoy as I know I'm getting some rest. What will it be tonight? Maybe a good 80s movie where Corey Haim and I can battle teenage angst, or a cooking show that makes me so hungry I wake up craving an exotic food I've never heard of!?

Speaking of craving, my buddy Jesse came by tonight with fresh Cactus Club Thai wings, something I've been craving all week. He and the family are heading back down south tomorrow after a week-long visit. I'm sad to see them go, but I'm looking forward to heading down that way to spend some time someday soon. Jesse and I always have good talks, talks that you only have with a few people in your life. He's always been like a brother to me, and I'm so proud of the life he has created for himself. He deserves it.

THE LUMP IN MY THROAT

I woke up at 8:00 a.m. this morning with Chad lying in bed next to me. For the past five days he's been sleeping on the couch, so when I felt the heat of his very missed body next to mine, I had to fight back tears. When did I get in such a fighting mode that I forgot how much I missed having him next to me?

I fell back asleep, dreaming that the past three weeks hadn't happened and that having Chad next to me, holding my hand, was normal again.

The dream was interrupted by groaning. He's nauseous and needs something to eat: toast and peanut butter. Groggy, dozy and overwhelmingly tired, I got up and made him his toast.

As I was falling back asleep I hear, "Ugh, there is too much peanut butter on this!" He headed to the kitchen to fix it.

I am so tired, but I offer to do it.

"No," he said sharply.

Moving to the couch, he asks for pillows.

His demands are simple, but his tone is hard. The lump in my throat grows a little more before I finally fall back asleep.

Later on, I drive him to clinic. Even if he is too tired to talk, it is nice to get out of the house together. I drop him off and go upstairs to the chest and respiratory center, where my dear friend Eva is. She is fighting a really big uphill battle right now, but regardless of the discomfort and drugs, she lights up the room.

I was emotional as I took the elevator up to see her, and within seconds of my arrival she keenly asked, "How is Chad!?"

We talked, and I read her the blog that Chad had written about how much she inspires him. I barely made it through the first paragraph before she was holding my hand, letting me cry as I read to her.

I'm holding my friend's hand while she fights for her life, and my boyfriend is just a few floors below, fighting a similar battle.

The two of them are kind, good people who don't deserve the hand they've been dealt. They fight tirelessly with optimism and positive energy. In my running clothes, in great health, I wonder what I did to deserve these two wonderful people and their love in my life.

Driving home from the clinic with Chad in the passenger seat, I asked him if there was any news.

"Meg, I just don't want to answer your questions. That's what the blog is for."

I don't think I need to explain in great detail how this made me feel. I didn't mean for it to happen, and I'm happy he didn't see my tears.

Focus. No tears. Fight. Don't think about it. But in retaliation, I'm going to turn up the Christmas music, even though it's only November. Take that.

At home, I heat up soup for him. "Don't scoop the soup, just pour it," he instructs.

As he naps later, I go to the gym and march on the step-machine like a mad woman, repeating: "This isn't Chad talking. He won't even remember the things he is saying to you. It's just the drugs." Repeat. "This isn't Chad talking. He won't even remember the things he is saying to you. It's just the drugs."

When I mention I'm going to do the laundry, he replies with, "You don't have to tell me everything you do. If you don't want to do it, don't."

It's just the drugs. I step in the shower, and as quickly as the water comes out the pipes, the tears come out of my eyes. I feel awful. I feel like I'm not helping. I feel like I'm annoying him. I feel like I'm a bother. I feel alone.

I know this isn't true. I know I'm not alone. I have wonderful, supportive people around me. I just feel alone in this relationship.

Once out of the shower, as quickly as he dozes in and out of consciousness, he slips in and out of his coldness towards me. "I would like a kiss, please. And can we play Connect Four now?"

That's all I need; one ounce of warmth and the lump in my throat starts to shrink.

THANKS, DAD

Chad's Blog
November 16, 2009

Today proved to be more challenging than most. I'm carrying too much fluid, and it's affecting me greatly. It was a big day, with multiple appointments that took me all over the hospital. My dad has been driving me to and from appointments during the week when Meg is working. He picked me up mid-morning and dropped me at the front of the hospital. He always asks if he can stay and help, but I hate inconveniencing people and often say no. Over the years I've spent much of my time in hospital alone, despite all the support I have, just because it's easier that way sometimes.

My first chore was to get a chest x-ray, so in I went to take my seat in the waiting room. As I waited, I knew I wasn't well and was going to have serious trouble getting through the day. A few moments later, I could see the outline of my dad walking toward me—I felt so relieved. First thing he did was get me an iced tea for my cotton mouth…so good. A father knows his son, and he ended up spending the whole day with me, wheeling me around the hospital from appointment to appointment. He's very patient, considering hospitals are the last place either of us want to be. He got me through this day like so many before.

I JUST WANT A DAY OFF

Another sleepless night.

At 1:30 a.m., I wake up from a short nap to silence. Chad has been shifting and moaning for the last hour—why is it so quiet? I look over at him: See stomach rise. See stomach fall. Phew. Ok. He's breathing. Back to sleep I go.

At 3:15, I awake to "Shiiit."

"What?"

"I'm bleeding. There is blood everywhere." I flick the light on and see that Chad's pillow and shirt are wet with blood. The weight of the tubes in his neck has made him bleed. His platelets are so low that his blood is unable to clot, and he's bled through his bandage.

We can fix this.

We get a spare cotton bandage and, like the nurse that I am not, I tape on some new gauze.

That should get us to the morning.

I get him sorted with his pillows. He dozes off.

At 4:45 a.m., Chad says, "Argh! I'm still bleeding! It's not working. I'm so uncomfortable." I peel myself off the couch and get a towel. The clinic opens at 7:00, so we only have a few more hours to get through before we can get his bandage fixed. I get a towel, prop him on the pillows, and just hope that something clots—just for a few hours.

Overtired, he whimpers, "I just want a day off."

At 7:00 a.m., we're up and out the door to get him to the clinic. I call work. I won't be able to make the 8:00 meeting. While Chad is getting cleaned up and adjusted, I go up to the 12th floor to see Eva. Similarly weak and dozing, she greets me with a warm smile, and I instantly feel less tired.

9:00 a.m. We get home and Chad curls up on the couch. He doesn't say it very often, so when he says, "I don't like being alone when I feel this bad," I call work and say I won't be coming in. I make sure Chad is comfortable before I make my way to bed for a nap.

It has not been a bad day, however. Aside from seeing Eva and being around to help Chad, the highlight of my day has been driving him to and from the clinic, because he was too tired to change the Christmas music I had playing on repeat.

CHAD'S BLOG

November 17, 2009

Last night I finally fell asleep for a few hours, only to wake up to a minor blood bath. The line in my neck decided to spring a leak. Meg and I did our best to clog it up until morning, when we hustled over to the clinic for repair. They bandaged me up, and the rest of the day has been a write off—for Meg, too.

I've been trying to sit up as much as possible with my head bobbing to the left, right, front and back, like a little kid in a car seat. So tired! I'm still waiting to hear from my doc if I'm going to start something soon. I'm back in tomorrow for a blood transfusion, and hopefully I will begin some cocktail of chemo and whatever drug they may or may not come up with.

We've offered to pay for the drug, which just might happen— it's all good, just give it to me. Cancer doesn't feel good, and there isn't much to do about that but get rid of it.

THE WARRIOR AND HIS ARMY

Megan's Blog
November 19, 2009

Someone recently told Chad that his name means "warrior." Talk about the right name for the right person.

My Chad, our Chad, is the ultimate warrior, fighting the ultimate battle. I'm sure he'd prefer to call himself George St. Pierre from UFC, but I'll stick with Warrior Chad for now.

I know Chad has been overwhelmed by the amount of people supporting him in his battle.

Family, friends, friends of friends, friends of family friends, friends I talk to every day, friends I haven't seen or heard from in years. I can barely express how appreciative I am of the army we have fighting with Chad. Fighting with me. Fighting with us.

For as long as I have known Chad, he has tried to be the lone warrior—fighting this battle in the privacy of his own head and body. *I can get through this, no need to call for backup.*

Not anymore. The last three weeks have proven that this battle is bigger than us.

I don't think either of us could get through this without your support and love. Thank you. Thank you for the early morning runs, letting me vent; midday visits to Chad while I'm at work; and the late night phone calls. Thank you.

CHAD'S BLOG

November 19, 2009

I lay emotionless and exhausted while they stick me, sit me up, sit me down, replace bandages, shoot saline up my nose, and fill me full of fluids while trying to take some out.

Almost every day I will be going into the hospital—one day for hemodialysis, the next for a multiple myeloma drug called Velcaid. I will begin taking high-dose steroids every few days with another drug called Thalidomide, which I will take daily.

This is not going to be easy with a bad heart and failing kidneys. I'm grateful something is happening, but frightened to be at this stage. Things happen so quickly, and right now there isn't the time or energy to be worried about much of anything. I am not myself and may not be for a little while to come. Having a shower and making it down to the car where my dad waits for me each day takes it all out of me. I'm having trouble holding a conversation, but deep down, I know what I'm doing. I'm preserving myself, storing up my energy so I can continue to fight another day.

SILENT NIGHT

I'm lying in bed while Chad prepares for another sleepless night in the living room. The lights are on, the TV is on, and he's sitting upright—all signs that it will be 3:00 a.m. or so before he starts dozing.

As I crawl into our cold, empty bed, I wonder what he thinks about while he stays awake all night.

Is he sad? Scared? Lonely?

I don't know. I don't even mind if he doesn't want to tell me, but whatever it is, I just want to make it better. I wish I could make it better.

Minutes after tucking myself in, he calls and asks if I can shut the computer off. Before doing so, I take a quick peek at what he wrote a little over an hour ago.

Maybe not the best thing for me to have read before going to bed, as now I am lying here with my eyes filled with tears and salt stains on my cheeks.

I know how tired he is, but seeing it written, and in words he only has the energy to type rather than speak, leaves me speechless. Speechless and helpless.

I don't have a magic wand to cure him of his suffering, or words to comfort him. I've tried, but like he said, deep down he knows what he is doing. That place is so deep that it's unreachable.

My eyes welled after reading his words, and when I kissed his forehead goodnight, I wanted to wrap my arms around him and say, "It will all be better soon."

But all I could muster was, "I love you".

I'm now back in our cold bed. I sleep on his side so that I don't roll over and put my arm here, finding that he isn't beside me. He doesn't know that I will cry myself to sleep tonight. It would be too much; he can't worry about both of us.

So with a wall between us and the mutter of the TV in the background, we both sit in silence.

I'm going to try to sleep. I'll close my swollen eyes, put my iPod on and dream of a magic wand.

WE'RE DOING OKAY.

Chad's Blog
November 24, 2009

For those of you keeping an eye out for him—it's been a few days since Chad has written, and I just wanted to write a quick update.

He has been really weak the past few days, spending long days in the clinic with his new treatment. The chemo cocktail and the clinic visits leave him with limited energy to do much else. Standing up is difficult, and he often needs my help getting off the couch; his dad takes him around the clinic in a wheelchair because walking is too tiring. Although he tries to eat, his stomach is too bloated and sensitive for much to fit in it.

He said this morning that he is ready to keep writing, so when he gets back from clinic tonight, he'll get on his blog again. However, his dad just called to say that Chad's being taken down to the emergency ward.

When he finished dialysis this evening, his blood pressure was really low, so they've taken him to emergency to get it sorted out.

I hope to hear more shortly. I hope to hear he is coming home. If not, I'll bring him his meds and some food, relieve his dad, and get through the night like we have done many times before. In the meantime, I just wanted to say we're getting by. One foot in front of the other, hour by hour, and we're doing okay.

THE SHOCKER

Megan's Blog
November 25, 2009

It's 3:30 a.m., and I'm sitting beside Chad's bed in the emergency room at VGH. I'm writing this on my smartphone with one hand, the other holding his while he sleeps.

I have a bizarre sense of calm as I watch him doze. His chest rhythmically rises and falls. His heart rate is a comfortable 94 beats per minute. I see his eyes roll open once in awhile, only to be followed by the small snores of a deep sleep. He squeezes my hand every few minutes. This means he loves me—it's a well-established gesture during those times when he is unable to talk.

I squeeze back, "I love you, too."

He did make it home tonight around 11:00 p.m., but only managed to rest on the couch for half an hour before he said he was having a hard time breathing. Five minutes after that, I was on the phone with his nurses, telling them he was going to have to come back in because his heart had started racing.

Trying to get him into his wheelchair became too much exertion to handle.

Here we go again.

911: "My boyfriend is a blood cancer patient. Yes, he's breathing. Yes, he is conscious. Yes, yes, no, no."

It took a little bit longer to get things sorted on the phone, as it was important that the paramedics knew to take him to VGH, where his files and docs were, rather than the closest hospital. The dispatcher complied, and so did the paramedics.

As we heard the sirens approaching in the background, I got Chad's meds together. After a knock at the door, a whole fleet of emergency personnel come through: three paramedics, two special unit people and two firemen—one in full "get the cat out of a tree" gear: helmet, jacket and boots.

They put the oxygen mask on Chad, and everyone takes turns asking the same questions.

"When?" "For how long?" "Why?" I'm watching them relay the information to one another, like kids playing Telephone at a birthday party. One says, "He has a high heart rate, on dialysis." Another says, "He has low blood pressure, blood cancer patient." The other says, "Heart palpitations, lung cancer patient."

Eventually he was scurried away with the uniformed fleet behind him.

Arriving at emergency, the monitors behind him recorded a heart rate of 190 beats per minute as we waited to be seen by the docs.

Once getting him on heart meds, his pulse slowed a little, but not enough. So they decided to shock him.

Oh god.

They quickly asked that I step out into the waiting room until they called.

I told him I loved him, and squeezed his hand. I said, "I know you love me, too."

He squeezed back and breathed, "loveyoutoo."

For that 15 minutes in the waiting room, I felt like I needed someone to check my pulse.

Thump thump. Thump thump. Shock is a good thing. I see them do it on TV all the time. It totally works. Right? Thump thump. Thump thump.

"Chad Warren!"

Thump thump. He's alive.

We came back to Chad's bed to see his face full of color rather than the grey it had been turning prior to jolting his heart full of electricity, and a lower, steadier heart rate.

My pulse returned to a steady beat as well.

He was able to talk a little, and tells us that what just happened was unbelievable. When I asked him if he was scared, he replied in true warrior fashion: "I just thought, this is it man, do or die. Here we go."

This guy is crazy.

The clock above his bed now reads 5:30 a.m., and I'm enjoying sitting with my boyfriend, who is alive and has once again proven that he is the toughest cookie I have ever met. He's trying to sleep, but he's uncomfortable and having sporadic panic attacks that leave him short of breath. The docs aren't too worried, as his stats are much better than when he came in. Hopefully one of these little pills kick in soon, and he will get further relief and rest.

As soon as he starts slipping into some drug-induced sleep, I'll go home and get some sleep of my own.

Goodnight and good morning.

DO OR DIE

Chad's Blog
November 25, 2009

After a 12-hour day at VGH, including four hours of dialysis, I got home only for my heart to bounce out of control once again, just like Halloween night. We made the decision, the ambulance was called and arrived.

Next thing I knew they were yelling, 'Code 3, obtain!' with sirens screaming on the way back to VGH.

Heart racing. No time this time, out came the shock pads. Everyone was confident. Megan was asked to leave. The last thing I said to myself was, "Do or die." And BOOM. They said I wouldn't remember, but I remember. I remember saying, "Holy shit." I don't remember the next 15 minutes, but my heart was stable.

Spent the last 24 hours in emergency, and have just been moved back up to the transplant ward...

SURRENDER

Megan's Blog
November 25, 2009

After last night's events, today has been far less "shocking." Chad spent the day in dialysis: getting meds, putting fluid in, taking fluid out, and on and on and on. His dad, Clark, stayed with him for most of the day while I went home to sleep.

Chad has spent the last 48 hours being so uncomfortable that his exhaustion seemed almost unbearable. They are giving him hydromorphine to help him rest.

When I arrived and asked how his day was, he muttered, "Ugh, whatever." He tried to tell me what the doctors had told him, but couldn't seem to find the words.

Later, Dr. Nantal came in. He asked how Chad was doing, and then came out with it: "I'm afraid it seems like your cancer has become resistant to all kinds of treatment now. Your counts are so high that the drugs are no longer making a difference."

Oh my god. This is it, isn't it? This is The Talk.

I sat on Chad's bed holding his hand as Dr. Nantal went on. Chad was emotionless. He didn't cry, didn't ask any questions; he just lay there, too uncomfortable to feel anything else.

I think he must have already known.

I don't remember what else was said. I just remember Dr. Nantal's hand on my shoulder. When he asked if I was okay, I nodded and blinked tears away.

When he saw my tears, Chad said, "I was hoping you wouldn't have to hear that."

My reaction was try-hard optimistic: "Well, you've heard this news before and been okay. There is nothing to say it won't happen again."

Then, as encouragement, I told him that Eva was going home today. His face lit up. I thought maybe that light across his face was because he and Eva were somehow connected, and hearing she was going home gave him hope. But the longer I thought about it, the more I realized that it wasn't because he had hope for himself. It was because he had hope for her.

I kept thinking about saying something like, "Never give up— it will be okay." But I knew better.

I knew that when Dr. Nantal said those words, this was it. It was time to accept. Not to be defeated, but to surrender.

I asked him why he wasn't crying, why he wasn't sad. He simply said, "Sometimes this is just how it is. I have fought for nine years. That's a long time. I'm really tired."

He looked exhausted.

Chad drifted in and out of exhausted sleep for the rest of the night, while his dad and I talked in the hall. He had already heard the news. I optimistically forecast what 'the end' might look like for Chad and me: I thought we might have a few weeks or months together to 'coast out' on maintenance drugs or something. We would go home, maybe sneak away for a weekend, enjoy each other while we could, talk again, kiss again and snuggle again. I thought we could find a beach somewhere and get married.

I couldn't have been more wrong.

Clark said that, given Chad's condition, the doctor was predicting that 'the end' would be in a few days. We were on the 15th floor, and it felt like my heart fell to the basement.

I cannot believe it has come to this. Our fairy tale is ending.

IT'S OKAY NOW

Megan's Blog
November 26, 2009

Today was another rough day.

Early this morning, the hospital called to say that Chad's heart had started racing again, and they were taking him down to the cardiac care unit.

I got to the unit to find Chad, on oxygen, with his heart rate back up at 190 beats per minute. He looked at me and breathed an update: "I've been hanging on for hours."

It looked like there were 15 mini-fists inside of his tummy, chest, throat and head, punching from the inside out. Punching to get out, punching to get free of the poisoned body. Fatigue was written all over him. His eyes were barely opening, and hand squeezes were all we could manage.

The doctors and nurses said that, because the medicine wasn't bringing his heart rate down fast enough, they were going to have to shock him again.

Okay. That's okay. He's done this before. It's okay. We're okay.

Our whole situation suddenly began to feel uncontrollable. Our lives were slipping from us quickly—and there wasn't a "What's next?" to lean on. I rubbed his legs and arms. We squeezed hands, and for the first time, I said something that I never thought I would ever have to say. "It's okay now. You can do whatever you want to do now."

He breathed back, "Thank you."

He waited another hour and a half before the anesthesiologists arrived to prepare him for the shocker.

We were asked to step out of the room. I went out into the hallway with Chad's mom, my mom and Bryn, who had just arrived. Their faces were puffy, evidence they had been crying on their way over.

One shock and it could all be over. There are no words in the English language to describe the feeling of waiting to find out if the person your world revolves around has died or survived. I watched his mom cry, my mom cry, hugging and waiting in the hallway.

But it didn't take long for Clark (who watched the whole thing) to come back and tell us, "It worked!" We came back into the room to see Chad drugged, more comfortable, and with a healthy, normal heart rate of 74 beats per minute.

I spent the rest of the day holding his hand, waiting for medics to arrive and bring him back upstairs to the familiar BMT ward. He's slept, he's snored, and he's spoken a little. The nurse brushed his teeth, and I gave him a wipe down.

His sister, Jen, is on her way from Edmonton, and we will do our damnedest to make sure nothing else happens until she gets here.

ALL THE TIME WE HAD LEFT

Outside the doors of the BMT ward, there is a little room with floral-patterned couches, Chatelaine magazines and soft, creamy lighting. That is where I sat, first with JJ and Katharine, and then later that night with Laura, as I told some of Chad's closest friends that he was at the end of his fight. Our warrior was dying.

There was nothing on the planet that could have ever prepared me for having to deliver news like that. I did the best I could to encourage them to enjoy his company, say what they wanted to say and enjoy the time left.

I knew that, when this was all over, I would experience a sadness I couldn't yet comprehend. But before then, soaking up every last drop of life was important.

When everyone had said goodnight, it was just Chad and I—alone for what might be one of our last nights together.

"Chaddy, I've been thinking." I rubbed scentless lotion on his back while he sat upright with his eyes closed. "I know this isn't what you and I had in mind, but you made the best of your life. We squeezed every ounce of opportunity from the time you were healthy—traveling, playing tennis.

349

"Of course…" I paused to compose myself, "Of course, I'm sad we won't get to be married or have childr…"

"Stop," Chad said clearly. "Stop—none of that. It's too hard."

I understood. It was too hard for both of us. We were not going to have the chance to spend forever together.

I changed topics. "Every time you had the energy, Chad, we zipped off for weekends to the Okanagan, we skied, went to Texas, traveled to Europe, spent time with our families—we've done so much together. Some people never get around to doing any of that!"

He nodded and rasped, "You're right."

I helped him lie back down and massaged his feet before I reminded him that I would be resting on the chair-bed if he needed anything.

It's all I can do. After a day of noise and battle, all we can hope for is that our warrior has a peaceful night.

HOW MUCH TIME DO I HAVE?

"Did I hear there was lemonade?!" It was 2:00 a.m., and the strain in his voice had lessened.

We had been trying to force some fluid in him for a while now, so the fact that he was craving his holy water was wonderful.

Lemonade, coming right up.

When his nurse came in, he mumbled that he was scared to fall asleep. Now, after watching him sleep all day, with his family here, I have realized it's because he feels safe when there are people around, and not when it's quiet and dark.

She reassured him that she would be coming in every five minutes to check on him while he sleeps, so he could just relax. His shoulders relaxed, the crease between his eyebrows smoothed out, and he drifted off.

The next time he stirred, I got out of my chair-bed and offered him the lemonade sitting on the bedside table. His voice was quiet, weak and raspy, but he was coherent. "How much time do I have?"

All four chambers of my heart felt like they joined together in one collective *thump*. I knew what he meant, but I clarified just in case there was the slightest chance that I had misunderstood him. "What do you mean, Chaddy?"

351

He gestured towards the clock hanging on the wall before cupping his forehead with his frail hands. "How much time do I have?"

What you mean is, how much time do you have before you die. Fuck.

In that room, in that moment, there was no light. I was suffocated and swallowed up by darkness.

"You've got time, Chad." As I answered him, even my bones felt soft. "You're not going to die tonight. Jen will be here in the morning to see you." I promised, "I will not let you die tonight."

Chad gave his best effort to nod before relaxing back on the pillow, "I just want to see my sister." Morphine whooshed through his body, and he asked that I keep talking. I found more stuff to talk about, without a single mention of time.

We woke around 7:30 a.m. to a gorgeous orange sunrise shining over a fog-covered city. It looked like what I imagine heaven might look like.

On my way to get more of Chad's meal replacement drink, his nurse stopped me in the hall to say, "I just wanted to let you know how much we all enjoyed Chad. Even in his sickest days, he was a pleasure to care for. He's a great, great man. It has been a real privilege to have known him."

It has been a privilege to be loved by him, too.

His phone buzzed from time to time, alerting him to text messages from his friends, cheering him on. I had been reading them to him the same way I read him any comments that were left on his blog. But today he handed me the phone and said, "It's time to turn it off now."

I asked if he was sure, but I already knew the answer.

There is a lot of medicated sleep happening right now, but my favorite part of the day is when he looks at me. There are seconds of clarity when we see each other and everything we've been together.

OUR WARRIOR SLEEPS

Chad's Blog
November 28, 2009

Our Warrior Sleeps

Chad Clark Warren passed away peacefully on Saturday night, November 28th, 2009, at 7:30 p.m.

He was comfortable, sleeping, and most importantly— surrounded by people who loved him.

THE UNIVERSE HAS STOPPED

Megan's Blog
December 1, 2009

It has taken me three days to write this. I don't know how to start. I don't know where to start. I don't know the words to use. There aren't any words that do this justice, there aren't any words that tell his story, and there aren't any words to explain how I feel.

I start writing sentences, and then I erase them. I keep checking my phone to see if that's him calling. I start thinking and have a hard time breathing. I close my eyes and I see him. I open my eyes and I wonder where he is. The universe has stopped completely.

I am numb.

That feeling of numbness I had on the night I found out this was the end...well, looking back, that was only a sliver of how I feel now.

Empty.

I keep going back to that afternoon, watching the final deterioration of his body, knowing that when Chad's family arrived, it would be his last day.

Chad, organized and disciplined to the very end, made sure his will was signed. It took him two separate tries to gather the strength to have a legible signature. Once finished, he asked, "What else is there to do?"

His sister gently cupped his hand in hers and compassionately spoke to him. "There is nothing left to do, Chad. Nothing left to say. You have done it all. We know how much you love us. We know you know we love you. We know you have fought hard. You don't have to say anything. It's okay to let go now."

As I held Chad's hands, he began repeating, "I'm ready, I'm ready now, hurry up. I'm ready." He thumped his fist on the bed beside him as if to express how serious he was.

It's okay, Chad. It's coming. It's okay.

The nurse brought in a sedative. We continued to tell him how much he was loved. We held his hands and kissed his cheeks. Then, as the IV dripped, he drifted into a deep sleep. With his family— our family—around him, I crawled into the bed beside him, held his hand, and positioned myself to have as much of my body touching the side of his as possible.

While I lay beside him, I whispered, "Drift to a beach somewhere in Australia, and I'll meet you there in March."

I hope he heard me when I said that he captured part of my soul five years ago, and that it will always belong to him.

For the rest of the afternoon, nurses continued to hang sedatives. Our close friends came to hold his hands and quietly said their goodbyes. I lie beside him, and between tears and "I love yous," I even fell asleep for a few minutes.

Hours passed, and his breathing continued to slow; there were signs that, while he heard what was being said to him, he had spoken his last words.

For a moment there was a break in the sedative, and he opened his eyes. He looked at me trustingly, and for those three seconds before he closed his eyes again, it was just him and I. That was the last time he saw me.

Around 7:30 that evening, his color started to change. Jen and I were on either side of him. Clark came into the room to tell us that he was going to take Chad's mom home. He said he would be back.

But within minutes, Jen put her hand on Chad's heart and quietly said, "I think he's going." She repeated it again more loudly, and my mom left the room to stop his parents.

Jen and I held his hands. She leaned close to him so he would be able to hear her quiet voice, and bravely repeated what she had said earlier, "It's okay, Chad. You've done good. You have done all there is to do. We love you. We know you love us, and it's okay."

And with that, and three little breaths, he slipped away. No suffering, no gasping, he just silently slipped away.

Thirty seconds later, my mom walked back into the room with his parents. I think he wanted it that way. Chad wouldn't have wanted his mom to see it.

I can't write about what happened afterwards. There isn't a way to explain that feeling. His family, sitting around him, holding his cold hands, kissing his grey cheeks, begging him to come back and wishing him comfort.

Outside, our friends had given us time to ourselves, waiting helplessly and patiently.

Eventually I gave him one last kiss on the forehead and left the room with my mom and friends around me. The ward's doors closed behind us as we walked towards the elevators, and there I crumbled. Collapsing to the floor like glass shattering on tile—I was in pieces.

357

I dropped down against the wall, sobbing, with my head in my hands.

It wasn't enough. My goodbye wasn't enough.

"I have to see him again. I have to see him just one last time." I stood up.

Nobody followed. I was met only by the sympathetic eyes of the teary-eyed nurses standing nearby. "Can I please go in again? Just quickly?"

Chad looked just as we had left him, only the bed had been laid flat. There wasn't a sheet over his face or anything that I hadn't expected to see. Just him.

Holding his hands to my face, I kissed him again and again, repeating, "I will always love you. I will love you forever."

EPILOGUE

The Last Kiss

When girls talk about their relationships, the subject of the first kiss invariably comes up. It's been almost six months since I've kissed Chad, but I remember our last kiss like it was the first thing I woke up to this morning.

It was in early November, when he was home between his week in H1N1 quarantine at the hospital and the week he went back to VGH to "get things under control."

He was uncomfortable, weak and unable to do much for himself. Our relationship at the time was mostly, "What can I get you?" and "Meg, can you pass me my pills, please?"

I was sleeping on the couch beside him for large portions of the night in case he needed help sitting up or wanted a blanket. But really I was there so that he wasn't lonely or scared.

During the day, we didn't talk very much.

It was a sunny afternoon, and he was sitting upright on the couch during what seemed to be a small window of relief. In his weakened voice he said, "Come here."

I went closer, standing by him, waiting for him to ask me to pass him something.

"No, closer, come here."

I kneeled in front of him.

He put his hands on my face and pulled me in for a kiss.

It had been so long since we had kissed. It had probably been weeks.

Chad and I had been kissing each other for five years, but there was something about this one: my chest filled with butterflies, like it was our first.

It lasted for what felt like minutes, and when it was over, I was weak in the knees.

We didn't talk much after: I resumed puttering around the apartment, and he flipped through the channels before dozing off. I remember looking over at him and realizing how much energy it took out of him to kiss me like that. How important it must have been to him to give me a kiss as memorable as that one was, transcending all the "Do you mind" and "Can you help me with" practical moments of our shared battle against his disease.

For those few minutes in that kiss, Chad wasn't sick, and I wasn't just there caring for him.

We were in love. It was pure and uncomplicated. Two people, in love, forever.

ABOUT THE AUTHOR

Megan Williams continues to live in the apartment she shared with Chad in North Vancouver, B.C., Canada.

Every day, she honors his memory by living her life as Chad lived: laughing often, loving deeply and travelling whenever she can.

Megan works for the B.C. Transplant Agency, and in her free time, does what she can to help Chad's family fulfill his goal of raising $1 million for multiple myeloma research.

To help, please visit chads1million.com.

To read more about Megan's journey, visit ourinterruptedfairytale.com

CPSIA information can be obtained at www.ICGtesting.com
Printed in the USA
LVOW12s0807100614

389382LV00002B/194/P

9 781493 712618